TRAUMA AND THE HUMAN CONDITION

Notes From the International Field

Anngwyn St. Just

Also by Anngwyn St. Just

Trauma: Time Space and Fractals : A Systemic Perspective on Individual,Social and Global Trauma, Createspace USA, 2012

A Question of Balance: A Systemic Approach to Understanding and Resolving Trauma, Createspace USA, 2009

Relative Balance in an Unstable World: A Search for New Models for Trauma Education and Recovery, Carl-Auer Verlag, Heidelberg,Germany,2006

In Translation:

Trauma: Tiempo, Espacio y Fractales
Editorial Alma Lepik, Buenos Aires, Argentina, 2012

Trauma: Una cuestion de equilibrio:Un abordaje sistemico para la comprension y resolucion,
Editorial Alma Lepik, Buenos Aires, Argentina, 2011

Equilibrio relativo en un mundo inestable: Una investigacion sobre Educacion de Trauma y Recuperacion, ,2nd ed.
Editorial Alma Lepik, Buenos Aires, Argentina, 2011

Sociales Trauma: Balance finden in einer unsicheren Welt
Kösel Verlag/Random House München, 2005

ISBN-13: 978-1484060490

ISBN-10: 1484060490

TABLE OF CONTENTS

December

2012:

January:

February:

March:

April:

May:

For John Bilorusky and the faculty of the

Western Institute for Social Research...

"You must go on. I can't go on. I go on."

(Samuel Beckett)

INTRODUCTION

"I yearn for my work because it always helps me make sense of things. For never was there a horror experienced without an angel stepping in from the opposite direction to witness it with me."

(Rainer Maria Rilke)

During the summer of 2011 I welcomed an invitation from Dr. John Bilorusky, founder and President of The Western Institute for Social Research in Berkeley, California to contribute material for their online web site focusing on topics having to do with education and social change. I came to WISR many years ago after completing my graduate studies in the humanities, art, history and languages, at the University of California at Berkeley. As much as I enjoyed a quiet life of study at UCB, my interest in the arts as reflections of social change led to a practical necessity for a career change as well. The subsequent transition, from those comfortably remote realms of academia to that of mental health professional, was eased by opportunities and support available from the WISR faculty and Dr. Bilorusky's astute advice and amazing patience. Since I was never all that interested in psychological studies emphasizing rats, mazes and statistics, I greatly benefited from WISR's individualized graduate study program, which combines academic theory and qualitative research with an emphasis upon interdisciplinary and cross cultural experience.

Writing soon became an important exercise in an ongoing effort to clarify and deepen my understanding of psychological trauma, as well as trauma education and recovery work. Since I am also a cultural historian, it was inevitable that previous art and historical studies would contribute to my contextual perspective; this eventually evolved into social and global trauma work. Research done for my master's and doctoral theses at WISR served as a basis for my first book, *Relative Balance in an Unstable World: A Search for New Models of Trauma Education and Recovery.* I continue to enjoy writing and am now able to devote more time to this since the closing of my private practice in the spring of 2001. Themes that I had begun to research at WISR eventually took shape in, *A Question of Balance: A Systemic Approach to Understanding and Resolving Trauma,* and more recently, *Trauma: Time, Space and Fractals: A Systemic Perspective on Individual, Social and Global Trauma.*

Leaving private practice also opened new opportunities for travel, teaching and work in vastly different cultural settings. These international experiences have added much richness and depth to my understanding of our human condition and the many challenges that we face during these trying times of rapid environmental and social change. WISR's invitation to join the online blogosphere came at an interesting time. During the summer of 2011, media hype and serious misunderstandings surrounding the Mayan calendar had given rise to an atmosphere of anticipation and dread, as we moved toward the apparently iconic year of 2012. While those unfulfilled apocalyptic memes continued to abound, there was no shortage of genuine and meaningful international events, which were being carried on into the new years of 2012, 2013 and beyond. Since this new project with WISR evolved from a series of monthly blogs (web+logs) the resulting contributions might now qualify as a "blook" (blog+book). Material contained within monthly entries "from the international field" differs from my earlier books, in that the focus now is almost entirely on current events and the trauma is social and global, rather than individual and family. For the most part, subjects included within this latest volume include topics of interest which arose within my own experience of international travel, social trauma seminars and training programs. While I seriously considered deleting accounts of my air travel tribulations, the fact is that what goes on in airports is often a microcosm of society at large.

For those unfamiliar with our subject, at this point it may be helpful to offer my working definition of trauma as it manifests in individuals and families, as well as social and global systems. It could be said that medical trauma results from injury to the physical body and psychological trauma from an injury to the psyche. However in reality, these two conditions often overlap since psychological shock and injury always has a physiological component which gives rise to patterns of somatically encoded stress. Trauma is a psycho-physiological and a potentially collective phenomenon which is not confined to one individual's, solely cognitive experience. In essence, trauma is all about an individual and/or collective response to overwhelming experiences that can lead to various levels of "broken connections". These broken connections can then lead to a fragmentation in relationship to self, loved ones and community; as in numbness, hyperactivity, disorientation in time and space and other forms of dissociation. Many overwhelmed individuals, families and communities also experience a profound sense of alienation, despair and fragmentation in relation to family, others and the larger matrix supportive of human life. This is similar to what Martin Buber called "a wound in the order of being". Trauma impacts our human ability to relate, learn, earn a living, and retain a capacity for intimacy and trust, as well as our ability to parent. Unresolved traumas, therefore, are often passed on to many subsequent generations. Traumatic experiences can overwhelm personal and professional relationships, entire families, communities, tribes and nations, and our planetary biosphere. Events in our distant past such as ice ages, titanic floods, polar shifts, asteroid impacts and other extinction level catastrophes, all qualify as global traumas. In modern times we have massive global trauma as a result of several nuclear meltdowns and the December 26th earthquake and tsunami which affected eleven countries and caused our Earth to wobble on its axis.

It is important to understand that individual, social, global and even political traumas often overlap and cannot always be conveniently confined to separate categories. Also important is the fact that all traumatized individuals and families are also integral parts of larger systems which connect to even larger patterns involving all of their relationships, culture and ancestral history. Even within apparently safe and familiar clinical settings, where it appears that therapists are working with one individual, they are in fact, engaging, influencing and being influenced by many interconnected and often unacknowledged larger systems. Ultimately, these largely unrecognized, interconnecting systems actually do extend all the way into society's most pressing and intractable problems; war, class struggle, racism, genocide, disease, violence, addiction, unemployment, poverty and so on... Any intervention made during an individual client's process will absolutely affect everyone else that he or she is connected to in the past, present and future. The more those of us in the healing and helping professions who are willing to become conscious of this larger interconnected reality, the more options we are able to bring to the challenge of understanding and resolving these many levels of trauma.

Several themes in social, political and global trauma that I followed in 2011 and 2012 involved many veils of secrecy and ongoing radiation dangers from nuclear accidents at Chernobyl, Fukushima Daaichi Complex and maybe others of which we are still unaware. I began writing about the aftermath of the USSR's, 1986 Chernobyl accident in 1992 during my first trip to Russia, and then about the Japanese disaster in March 2010. While one may wonder why I tend to go on and on about these events, our reality is that the disasters themselves go and on, with no end in sight. Obtaining accurate information about these greatest catastrophes of modern times has been an ongoing challenge due to overt lies, cover-ups, media black outs and a pervasive, complicit atmosphere of collective denial. The information subsequently presented here was mainly derived from alternative media and foreign press and offered from a conviction that endangered populations have a right to potentially life-saving information. Reliable facts, made immediately available, can greatly improve our chances of minimizing hazardous exposure, maximizing options for health and safety and taking precautions to enhance and protect both our immunological defenses and our DNA.

In a way, this blook could have been given a title something like: *"In Order to Avoid Panic"* since this rationale of denial is employed over and over again for withholding, minimizing and distorting vital information. We often hear that what we know to be life-threatening events, "present no danger to human health". In fact, variations upon this Orwellian message accompany most public service announcements about events that are quite obviously dangerous to both public health and safety. We also find an almost comical over-use of such canned phrases as "minimal risk", with lethal substances described as "mild irritants" or "low toxicity", and now the latest Australian version, "of no significant concern". By now, the awake and aware have figured out that such banal reassurances most likely indicate the certain presence of significant dangers that most definitely warrant immediate attention.

While nuclear events were a dominant theme in 2011-12, this time frame contained no shortage of noteworthy developments reflecting various aspects of our rapidly changing, all too human condition. As long as we are living here on Planet Earth, in many ways a difficult as well as beautiful habitat, we would do well to accept that trauma is and always has been an integral part of our *homo-sapiens* experience. At this point in our evolution it is simply not possible to "trauma-proof" or vaccinate our species against the kinds of overwhelming experiences that can lead to trauma. For now, our best option is to gather resources conducive to mental, physical and spiritual health and also to promote resources and resiliency. My understanding of resources includes those people, places, things and experiences that relieve anxiety and tension and reinforce one's sense of strength, purpose and positive connection to life. Resources can also be found in positive memories and dreams that provide a sense of safety, comfort and support during times of difficulty and pain.

One can never have too many resources and most of us have more resources than we realize. During my clinical experience, I observed that those who have a strong positive connection to both parents, entire family of origin, ancestors and cultural roots, possess the greatest capacity for resiliency, as well as an ability to adapt and prevail within very difficult circumstances. This observation makes sense if one considers the basic biological reality, that life itself is given through mother and father and that this came down to them through their ancestors. Respect and an aware connection to this basic reality, on the biological and soul level, offers a sense of strength and also serves as a powerful resource in the face of adversity and the uncertainty of the future.

July
2011

Mexico City

"Mexico City is the absolute center of an absolutely centralized country. It is the absolute power center, the axis of government and finance and culture and the nation's history, the umbilicus of the Mexican universe...The nation, in fact, has taken its name from the city that rules it. (John Ross)

While I have been here many times, and for many reasons, this is my first visit to *El Centro de Constelaciones Familiares* now in the beginning stages of their new master's degree program in Systemic Social Solutions. My seminar on Systemically Oriented Social Trauma was attended by local therapists and other Mexican citizens deeply concerned about their deteriorating infrastructure and the escalating violence of their ongoing drug wars. British journalist, Ed Vulliamy, author of *Amexica: War Along the Borderline* (2010,) describes the violence perpetrated by multiple and fiercely competitive narco-cartels as "warfare for the 21st century". A nightmare of ongoing conflicts has claimed nearly 40,000 lives, mostly civilians, generated arms trafficking scandals and endless debates over military and para-military solutions. It has led to the questioning of the efficacy of decriminalizing drugs. While one usually thinks about war as something fought between people with causes, Vulliamy maintains that this conflict is about tribal dynamics among rival *narco-trafficante* gangs; territory, profit and the glorification of the cruelest forms of sadistic violence. While these modern day killers tout and even post their atrocities on You Tube, this cult of ritual savagery has very deep roots in a history of place; pre-Columbian cultures, and a quasi-Catholic cult of Santissima Muerte (Holiest Death).

In this regard, American ex-pat, John Ross's. *El Monstruo: Dread and Redemption in Mexico City* offers much to ponder. This fascinating volume was written from his window in the creepy old Hotel Isabel in the historic Colonial Quarter where he has lived since the earthquake of 1985, which crushed nearly 30,000 lives. Ross's history of this mile high city, surrounded by 34 volcanoes, covers four million years of upheaval. Beginning with geological origins, he continues on to Pre-Colombian, Aztec-Mexican cultures in their "City of Smoking Hearts and Flowers"; subsequent genocides, the complexities of colonialism and revolutions, on up until a Swine Flu panic of 2005. Mexico City has never been a particularly peaceful place. *El Monstruo's* history of violence woven together with the spectacular and often mysterious beauty of pre-Columbian cultures is evident throughout the National Museum of Anthropology. I discovered this national treasure many years ago as an undergraduate student of art and architectural history and endeavor to re-visit their Aztec Sun Stone and other impressive displays whenever I return. In light of the recent history of ritual violence and torture as part of drug-gang culture, it is interesting and instructive to be able to trace these very similar cruelties to many and various figures depicted throughout this truly awe inspiring museum. While I seriously doubt that sadistic gang members are roaming these national exhibit halls in search of inspiration, I do sense a deep rooted connection to this aspect of their cultural roots, which is overlooked by simplistic solutions of a political or economic nature. In the long run, a study of Mexican history suggests that any proposal which ignores these systemic elements is not likely to succeed.

Republic of Chile

"Write what must not be forgotten" (Isabel Allende)

We have bone cold, freezing, mid-winter temperatures here in Santiago de Chile and the mountains surrounding the city are completely white. In recent years, this troubled country has been relatively stable after decades of dark times and political trauma. On September 11, 1973, a U.S. assisted (Nixon/Kissinger/CIA) military coup overthrew democratically elected President Salvador Allende and installed the notoriously brutal dictatorship of General Augusto Pinochet. Questions regarding President Allende's death by murder or suicide remain unresolved. Pinochet's militaristic regime soon established his Chilean led *Operation Condor* among six other South American dictatorships. Soon thereafter, a troubled era of human rights violations was rapidly underway; including intimidation, torture, political assassinations, concentration camps, kidnappings and thousands of "disappeared". Former American Ambassador to Chile, Jon Dinges' account in, *The Condor Years: How Pinochet and His Allies Brought Terrorism to Three Continents*, offers a much needed and major contribution to a still clouded historical record. It is important to understand and appreciate that this country is still engaged in a complicated process of coming to terms with this aspect of their past. In January 2010, then President Michelle Bachelet inaugurated a new *Museum of Memory and Human Rights* in downtown Santiago. Ms. Bachelet had spearheaded this project as a survivor who had been detained, tortured and driven into exile during Pinochet's dictatorship. Her own father died as a result of government sponsored cruelties. This national museum now serves as "an invitation to reflect upon attacks made on life and dignity from September 11, 1973 until March 10, 1990 in Chile".

August of 2010 brought a storm of national and international media attention to Chile and the plight and dramatic rescue of 33 miners, trapped 700 meters underground for nearly two months. Not surprisingly, their story is soon to become a Hollywood film. I was puzzled that this subject never came up during my social trauma seminar. Colleagues later explained that the silence likely arose from much local resentment toward the international media, which simultaneously ignored the plight of the 33 Mapuche hunger strikers imprisoned, because they protested government incursions into their sacred lands. Thousands took to the streets in Santiago in support of the Mapuche cause, and eventually a compromise was achieved.

Chile's long, narrow and greatly diverse landscape contains some of our planet's most spectacularly beautiful and also seismically active territory. Last February an earthquake with a magnitude of 8.8 caused considerable damage and social unrest in and around Santiago. Further south there was massive devastation in their capital city of Concepcion and along several stretches of coastline, where entire communities were suddenly washed away by tsunami. These catastrophes shook local populations on a number of levels, including the psychological, with a resultant upsurge of previous and unresolved traumas. My arrival soon after was heartened by a greeting from the wife of newly elected President Sebastian Pinera, who had been invited to my public lecture on earthquake related trauma and the subsequent workshop on Natural Disasters: Trauma and Recovery. Although Señora Pinera was too busy to attend, she graciously sent a warm welcome and a "big hug".

Now, in July 2011, the Puyehue volcano in the southern Andes, dormant since 1960, has exploded a massive, ash laden, mushroom cloud six miles high into the upper atmosphere.

Thousands were evacuated from surrounding communities and a volcanic plume continues to disrupt air travel as far away as Australia and New Zealand. Strong winds carried massive amounts of ash further across the Cordillera Range on over into Argentina. Flights in and out of Buenos Aires were continuously interrupted. From the internet, friends far down in Patagonia sent spectacular photos of their landscape in San Carlos de Bariloche. Several of these images brilliantly captured the shock and terrors of sudden thunder and daylight-darkened skies streaked with blood-red lightning on a scale and intensity never before seen. For days, an ongoing rain of ash covered their picturesque town, lake and forest landscape with several feet of what looked something like pale grey snow....deeply disturbing, almost apocalyptic and definitely surreal. My workshop scheduled for the following week in Neuquen "the gateway to Patagonia", was cancelled since all regional airports were closed....indefinitely.

Argentina

"In government, one actress is enough" (Evita Peron)

Buenos Aires is my professional home in Latin America. For over eight years now, I have occaisionally been living here and offering seminars and public lectures in the southern hemisphere. At first, being down here was somewhat disconcerting since their "Man in the Moon" looks unfamiliar, our lunar satellite appears upside down and backwards, night sky constellations are quite different and the seasons are reversed. Nevertheless, I was eventually able to re-orient. This recent visit was especially gratifying since it included a completion of my two year, systemically oriented social trauma modules, and an opportunity to congratulate students who have finished this training. Their last module was about burnout...also known as "compassion fatigue." Ideally, this module would be offered at a beginning and not the end of trauma training curricula because it is the absolute number one reason why we cannot keep people actively engaged within our field. Often, healing and helping professionals rush headlong into trauma work because they want to help and be of service. Just as often, they are woefully ill-prepared for oncoming and inevitable real life challenges. Many of these well intentioned souls soon find themselves caught up in complex and overwhelming situations where they are in too deep without adequate skill, experience, supervision or other appropriate support. Overcome by overwhelm, they eventually drop out. I began to address this issue in my first book, *Relative Balance in an Unstable World: A Search for New Modules of Trauma Education and Recovery* (also available in Spanish and German).

Those of us well experienced in trauma work know and understand the seductive powers of intensity and crisis, and that special comfort of being in the presence of someone whose pain is greater than your own. In some ways, crisis also serves as a kind of emotional undertow and pressure equalizer; where outside pain serves to offset and balance whatever pain still rests inside oneself. This process, however, has a tendency to become cumulative, whereby the pain of others continues to become compounded with one's own. The danger here is that gradually, or even suddenly, there can develop an ever increasing need to search out and find ever larger fields of intensity and crisis. It is not difficult to imagine how a process such as this can prove disastrous for intimate partnerships and the pragmatic routines of ordinary family life; and how easily trauma specialists can become isolated from their loved ones. Over time, these patterns of ongoing intensity, overwork and isolation can also lead to serious health problems, as the body breaks down from ongoing stress and lack of maintenance. It has been my experience that what one chooses as a profession, way to earn a living or as a serious hobby, often has to do with a conscious or unconscious desire to heal some unfinished business left over from previous generations. At times this can manifest as a conviction that one is destined to carry out some form of personal mission. These missions that stem from entanglements with previous generations or other members of one's family system, often contain a decidedly driven quality. For those facing burnout or wishing to prevent this, it could be useful to ask, "Who or what am I trying to save? For whom or for what am I trying to atone? What is unfinished or unbalanced in my family system, and does my choice of work have anything to do with that?" These questions and concerns are not intended to discourage those who might be interested in or already engaged in trauma work. The intent here is to raise awareness of some of the more obvious pitfalls and to encourage anyone interested in healing, helping and trauma work to undertake a commitment to seriously pursue their own inner work as part of any effort to be of genuine service to others.

August 2011

Venezuela

"Venezuela has changed forever" (Hugo Chavez)

Political Trauma was the title of my workshop
here. In recent days, news of President Hugo
Chavez has been featured in much of the
international media along with speculations
about his health, possible successors and
subsequent power struggles should he succumb
to a very serious cancer. The current situation
here brings to mind thoughts and memories of
my 2010 seminar in Caracas. I was invited by
Dr. Marie-Dolores Paoli who is known
throughout South America for her pioneering
work with Indigo children. Dr. Paoli and her staff
suggested a topic of political trauma, which I
resisted for a number of reasons, including the
fact that I had never offered a seminar on that
subject and am also unwilling to engage in any
partisan agenda. Nevertheless, they insisted on

this topic and after some lengthy negotiations, I agreed to undertake this new challenge. Dr. Paoli then announced that some of her Indigo children would be attending my seminar, along with their parents, and this was also a new and very unexpected experience. The capital city of Caracas is a dangerously violent place with one of the highest accident and homicide rates in Latin America. During this seminar it soon became apparent that much of the population lives with a constant, all pervasive, feeling of threat. While there are many obvious reasons for this, such as poverty, overcrowding, drug addiction and trafficking; it is important to understand the many layers of complexity that have shaped Venezuelan history.

From a systemic perspective, together with other parts of Central and South America, many levels of this multi-racial society cannot be understood apart from the ongoing legacies of colonialism. A thorough account of this historical reality is available in Eduardo Galleano's, now classic,

Open Veins of Latin America. From a systemic perspective, specific personalities and political leaders are not the problem, but rather symptoms of the problem...or problems. This is difficult to accept for those who wish to place singular blame on one particular leader or political party, without reflecting upon the underlying dynamics that brought them into positions of power.

Soon after my return to Argentina I received a surprising and deeply moving letter from one of my workshop participants; an eleven year old boy who identifies himself as an Indigo child. "Jose" thanked me for coming to Caracas, and overcoming my initial reluctance to address the topic of political trauma. He wrote that it was important for him and the other children that they were welcomed into my seminar, and that this was also an acknowledgement for them and their parents, that Indigo children actually do exist.

Jose continued on to share his own perspective on a remedy for ongoing violence in Venezuela which is translated here from the Spanish.

"Do you know what is needed in each Venezuelan home? Even if it seems simple...A pleasant space inside the dwelling where pastel colors show the colors of our ancestors, a nice "taparita" (painted gourd) decorated with the savors of a fruit, a rain forest tree stick to honor the indigenous, a Spanish mantilla in the drawers of the women to honor the Spaniards, to also wear some pearls, place a drum, and a wooden tray to honor our African slaves, so that our homes would have the balance of truth with joy. We need to forgo the proclaiming of our patriotic souls and devote ourselves rather to the soul of being human, honor our creator and avoid religious images that call upon pain and darkness."

This, in short, is a call for every home to become "a temple of peace". Whether or not one believes in the existence of the Indigos, this "child's" letter offers much for reflection.

Trauma and Organizations

"This is still open terrain to be explored"
(Jan Jacob Stamm)

My Dutch colleague Jan Jacob Stam, author of, *Fields of Connection*, a book about organizations from a systemic perspective, has recently begun to explore the topic of organizational trauma. In a recent article published in the June 2011 edition of, *The Knowing Field: International Constellations Journal*, he asks if organizations as well as people can be traumatized. According to a recent, highly controversial remark by Republican presidential candidate Mitt Romney, "Organizations are people", at least according to the corporate friendly U.S. Supreme Court Justices. Jan Jacob however, is more interested in system than politics and the question of "what exactly is traumatization"? Can a department be traumatized? An organization does not have a body, but can an organization have symptoms as if it were a body? Is there such as thing as a traumatic field? In this exploration Jan Jacob is working with a definition of trauma as something that can happen as a result of shock, fragmentation and "broken connections", and when a system is so overwhelmed that it is not able to bounce back to its original strength. Symptoms mentioned by people in his organizational workshops include: a rigidity (freezing?) of the organization when proposing change or a new direction as though it was stuck somewhere in time, a gulf between older and newer employees, lack of flow between various divisions or between the organization and the outside world.

A case like this presented itself in Holland. During a serious agricultural epidemic, thousands of animals had to be killed so that the virus would not spread. Afterward, there remained a deep gap between the agricultural ministry and a large part of the farming communities. One also suspects trauma when a majority of members are focused on the past rather than the present or future. Jan Jacob's next questions therefore are "what helps" and "how to restore resiliency"? Following my research which indicates that people who are most connected to their roots are less likely to be traumatized and also more likely to rebound in situations of adversity, Jan Jacob put this to the test during work with an organization in Mexico City. In this case with "roots", the issue is: the original purpose of the organization, social and historical issues contributing to the distress, and the history of place where the business is located. His client was the manager of a Mexican bank where the resistance to having a call center appeared to be a racial issue. Lowest paid employees are usually of Indigenous origin, and the challenge became to find ways for them to connect with their roots within a commercial context. Jan Jacob also wonders, "what happens when a company is "uprooted" and moves to another location? What happens when you outsource production to a lower wage country? Is there something like survivor guilt that happens with employees remaining after massive layoffs and abrupt terminations?" As he makes clear, at this point, he has more questions than answers and his international explorations are ongoing.

While organizational trauma is not my specialty, I have also been wondering about this topic with questions such as: "what is going on with a French Telecom Company, that 23 employees have committed suicide within an 18 month period? What will be the consequences of lies, cover-ups and public health hazards promulgated by Tokyo Electric Power Company during and after their ongoing Fukushima nuclear disaster? And, how will this ongoing global disaster impact the corporate owned nuclear power industries? What will be the impact of telephone hacking allegations within Rupert Murdoch's family owned publishing empire?"

Many more of these kinds of questions remain to be explored and I look forward to learning more from Jan Jacob Stam's ongoing experiences.

September 2011

Japan: Hiroshima to Fukushima and Beyond...

'This is Japan's most severe crisis since the war ended in 1945" (Prime Minister Naoto Kan)

The prophetic words of J. Robert Oppenheimer, "father" of the atomic bomb, "I have become Shiva, Destroyer of Worlds", have become something like a mantra for an ongoing nightmare of nuclear destructive capability. The nuclear genii unleashed as an agent of mass destruction, continues to challenge any illusion of human control. Following the 1945 destruction of Hiroshima and Nagasaki, one wonders what the post-war Japanese were thinking when they began construction of 54 nuclear reactors on the coasts of their island nation located along the Pacific Ring of Fire. Roughly the size of California, the Japanese archipelago, crowded with 127 million people, is situated along a junction of four mobile tectonic plates and experiences some of our planet's strongest earthquake and tsunami activity. Ah, but there was money to be made, lots and lots of money. These Japanese reactors were built with political help and heavy investments from British and American companies; US Navy designed reactors, built by GE and Westinghouse using Japanese contactors.

And then, on March 11, 2011, Japanese history was again altered by yet another nuclear nightmare, an undersea quake with a reported magnitude of 9.0 which occurred off the coast of Northeastern Japan. Like the massive wave in Hokusai's 19th century iconic wood block print, a deadly tsunami easily rolled over shoreline defenses and severely damaged several nuclear reactors in the Fukushima Daaichi complex. Within hours, these reactors suffered a series of equipment failures, fires, three hydrogen explosions, our world's first triple meltdown, and a core "melt through" of radioactive magma through secondary containment vessels.

So now, we've entered the realm of global trauma, as these irreversibly damaged power plants continue to release massive amounts of deadly radioactive materials into our biosphere. Hot particles now enter the atmospheric Jetstream. They seep into the groundwater and long ranging ocean currents, the local landscape and the planetary food chain; which involves all plant and animal life. Fukushima Daaichi is now the worst nuclear disaster in the history of humanity and it is far from over.

Accurate information is hard to come by via any mainstream media, because of the pervasive political power of the nuclear industry. It is a fact that several major corporations that are heavily invested in nuclear power also own large portions of mainstream media outlets. The Japanese, British and American governments have withheld information, "in order to avoid panic"; resulting in a public relations success and a public health disaster.

It is important to remember that radioactivity from the 1986 Chernobyl disaster, which only burned for 10 days, has permanently contaminated an area of 77,000 square miles. The radioactive plume from that one reactor extended far beyond the borders of Ukraine and resulted in millions of deaths from lethal cancers, sudden heart failure, genetic damage, birth defects and other related conditions. The ongoing, uncontrolled multiple meltdowns of Fukushima's reactors are a far worse catastrophe and large areas of Japan are becoming uninhabitable.

What does this mean for the rest of the world? Public education is urgently needed since lethal radiation is odorless and invisible and therefore easy to deny and ignore. There will always be those who seek safety in a belief that "what we can't see won't hurt us", and also those who don't want to know anything about things that they believe they can do nothing about. And, Japan is after all, "so far away". Fortunately, much of our alternative media, internet sources and foreign press (many have English language editions) are awake, and aware of this planet-wide danger. Several provide vital information updates and advice from experts in radiation and nuclear medicine as to what one can do to minimize risk and exposure. The danger of radioactive contamination is very real, especially to the unborn, very young, and immune impaired. Fortunately, it is also known that dietary and lifestyle changes and specific supplements can provide important options for minimizing risk.

Another September Eleventh

We are behind you. You are the leader.
(General Pinochet to Kissinger in the same meeting)

It has been my observation both as a historian and a clinician, that traumas tend to happen on the anniversary of other traumas. Terrorists know this and often strive to orchestrate catastrophic events on an anniversary of previous social and political traumas. These specifically dated events are designed to draw attention to something unresolved. On a national scale, Americans would see this manifest in the horrors of September 11, 2001 which can be seen as both the cause and result of other cycles of violence. If we choose to highlight the use of historical events rather than transitional dates to delineate historical eras, then this now totemic date of September 11,

2001 serves to mark the inception of our new millennium. The second passenger plane, as most everyone knows, was the one that hit the World Trade Center's second tower. And, it was this second aircraft, as Martin Amis wrote a few days later, that utterly annihilated any hope that what was happening, on that clear Tuesday morning, might have been nothing more serious than a tragic aviation disaster. For the thousands in the South Tower, this second plane meant the end of everything. For the rest of us, its terrifying glint was a harbinger of change. Archetypal images of collapsing towers were soon imprinted on the collective psyche. A series of events which took place on or around that date is now compressed into digital shorthand as: 9/11. Aided by our always complicit media, politicians lost no time in fetishizing this terrifying footage into a justification for a policy of endless "war on terror".

As we now know, attacks involving the airlines, World Trade Center and the Pentagon were immediately blamed on Islamic terrorists, and a "clash of civilizations". This purported truth, laced with religious overtones, subsequently served to justify wars in Afghanistan, Iraq, Pakistan, and now Libya; as well as an ongoing policy of endless and expanding global aggression. The events of 9/11 also spawned the Gestapo-like Department of Homeland Security, along with the authoritarian TSA and the ongoing and increasing public and private surveillance in nearly all walks of life. All in the interest of "public safety".

Our day of infamy, and the loss of sovereign America–as–sanctuary, was also the eleventh anniversary of a "New World Order" speech that George Bush Senior, former CIA director and the then President of the United States, made to a joint session of Congress. On this occasion he chose to announce his administration's decision to go to war with Iraq in the First Gulf War. It is also interesting to note that construction of the Pentagon, one of the 9/11 targets, began on

September 11, 1944. September 11th has a tragic resonance in the Middle East as well. On that date in 1922, ignoring Arab grief and outrage, the British government issued a mandate in Palestine which promised European Zionists a national home for Jewish people. This, in turn set the stage for wars, terrorist attacks, and ongoing conflict. Again on September 11th, a Palestinian terror group named Black September took hostages at the Munich Olympics and killed eleven Israeli athletes.

Internet rumors have suggested that September 11th echoes dates in 1683 of the Battle of Vienna, considered to be a final turning point in the conflict between the forces of the Christian West and Islamic Ottoman Empire. In September of 1697, Ottoman Turks lost a large amount of East European territory after another devastating defeat by the Austrians. However, exact dates of these temporal correspondences cannot be confirmed given that dates of the Islamic lunar and Western, Gregorian solar calendars are not the same. Another clash of civilizations began on September 11, 1906 when Mahatma Gandhi announced plans for a non-violent resistance to British rule. And then, on another Tuesday, September 11th, President Nixon, Henry Kissinger and the CIA backed an aerial bombing and coup which resulted in the overthrow and death of Chile's democratically elected President Salvador Allende. The subsequent regime of General Augusto Pinochet was responsible for the "disappearance" of thousands of people, firing squads, concentration camps, and torture chambers that opened throughout the country.

Now in 2011, as Chile marks the anniversary of their September 11th, Chilean writer Ariel Dorfman discussed this event in a video interview with Amy Goodman's *Democracy Now*. Recently recognized as one of Latin America's greatest writers, Señor Dorfman sadly lamented the tragic consequences of our vengeful cowboy diplomacy.

"Chile reacted to the terror that was inflicted upon us, with non-violent resistance. In other words, for instance, we did not go and bomb Washington because Washington had ordered and helped to create the coup in Chile. On the contrary, we created a peaceful revolution against Pinochet. If you contrast that to the United States, to what Bush did as a result of this very small band of terrorists, the results have been absolutely terrible. If this was a test – and I think great catastrophes are always tests of national will – alas, the United States has failed that test terribly. If you look, I mean of the results of September 11, 2001, it has been just terrible what has happened."

While it is not at all clear as to how many of the events of September 11th were consciously or unconsciously planned for that date, or were a result of pure coincidence; this long fractal is likely to continue given the lingering doubts, distrust and animosities surrounding the tragedies of 2001.

October 2011

Fukushima: Trauma and the History of Place

"It is hard to be an individual in Japan"
(Haruki Murakami)

It is the nature of war and also human nature that what has remained unfinished will pass on to the next generation in one form or another. History of place often plays a role in these traumatic repetitions. Many cultures believe that places have something like "fields of memory". From a systemic perspective, Japan's relationship to nuclear energy predates the events of Hiroshima and Nagasaki. In Martin Fackler's article in the *NY Times*, September 9, 2011, "Fukushima's Long Link to a Dark Nuclear Past", it comes to light that during the latter months of World War II, Imperial soldiers forced local school children to mine uranium ore from a nearby foothill in Fukushima Prefecture. This ore was then sent to Military Factory 608 which refined it into yellow cake. Children were put to work by the military since all men had been sent away to war. These children were told that "with the stones that you are digging up, we can make a bomb the size of a matchbox that will destroy all of New York". Two of the 130 schoolchildren used to mine uranium ore, Kuniteru Maeda and Kiwamu Ariga, now in their eighties, became schoolteachers and later pooled their money to self-publish their experiences on this wartime bomb project. In recent years Mr. Ariga has begun to tell his story to local schoolchildren who are often shocked that their country also tried to manufacture an atomic bomb. Furthermore, he tells them, "I have no doubt that Japan would have used it, if it had succeeded".

Mr. Ariga is now angry at a parallel he sees between that bomb project and Japan's current nuclear crisis. The main similarity, he says, is that in both cases, the population was deceived by what he called hubris-filled *leaders*. This perspective is shared by Japanese journalist

Yoichi Shimatsu, former editor of *The Japan Times* and lecturer from Tsinghua University (*Global Research*, April12, 2011). He was not surprised when the Tokyo Electric Power Company and Japanese officials initially responded to their nuclear crisis with denial, outright lies, media control and other attempted cover-ups. No foreign nuclear engineers or Japanese journalists were permitted entry into the damaged reactor structures. Mr. Shimatsu believes that confused and bumbling responses, miscommunications and half-baked reports coming from the Fukushima Complex were likely driven by a much darker agenda. In his view, the most logical explanation for this smoke and mirrors performance, is that industry and government agencies are scrambling to prevent discovery of atomic bomb research facilities hidden within Japan's civilian power plants. Enrichment of uranium for nuclear warheads is forbidden under Japanese constitutional law and the terms of the Non-Proliferation Treaty. Mr. Shimatsu also maintains that this hidden nuclear weapons program is a ghost in the machine now reflecting the violence inherent in an earlier secret program. If true, these new revelations about Japan's wartime and recent attempts to manufacture nuclear weapons add another dimension to the ongoing crisis in Fukushima prefecture.

Alaska: Arctic Ozone Depletion

"We're looking at Earth science observing our planet. Also, space science looking at the ozone in the atmosphere around our Earth....And on a human level, using ourselves as test subjects"
(Allison Gibney, Physician)

Fairbanks, Alaska: This is my first trip to Alaska, "The Last Frontier" according to many local license plates. It feels somehow satisfying to be traveling this far North since I spend so much time down in the southern regions of our planet. In some geomantic traditions there is a belief that a person can refresh their energy by traveling in vertical, as opposed to horizontal directions, as this brings a kind of balance. I can now imagine that there might be some truth to this ancient teaching. Fairbanks sits at 64 degrees north latitude.   Just today, we have received disturbing news from zones even further north, all the way up into the Arctic

Circle. An enormous hole in Earth's protective ozone layer has suddenly torn open and continues to expand. Even more troubling, we have reports that this new hole is the first of its kind and largest ever recorded in the Northern Hemisphere. This does not bode well. Reports of an 80 percent loss of ozone in our upper atmosphere, with potential to expose everyone and everything on the planetary surface to harmful ultraviolet B rays from the Sun, should be cause for world-wide concern. Air masses exposed to ozone loss above the Arctic tend to drift southward and may affect the middle latitudes. Ultraviolet B rays have been linked with skin cancer, cataracts and damage to the human immune system. These rays can also produce adverse effects in marine life and vegetation which could reverberate throughout the global food chain. Damage to tiny phytoplankton could also have world-wide consequences since they play a crucial role in regulating atmospheric levels of carbon dioxide.

Almost every web site that carried this story offered a variety of reasons for this unexpected phenomenon. As recently as nine years ago, the World Meteorological Society assured us that the Arctic would never experience an ozone hole since it lacked a polar vortex and the cold temperatures necessary to produce such a breach. Now, we are asked to believe that this sudden anomaly was produced by the 2010/2011 winter, a stratospheric, icy cold, wind pattern known as the polar vortex. Mainstream media stories hold that this unusually strong polar vortex, led to prolonged sub-zero conditions. These unusual conditions lasted for months and this in turn created ideal conditions for ozone-destroying chlorine compounds to eliminate the ozone. Now, what caught my immediate attention was the fact that this anomalous, Arctic ozone hole opened suddenly in March and April and is undergoing a process of continuous expansion.

For a systemically oriented global traumatologist, the obvious question is, "What happened suddenly in March of 2011?"

Well, in March of 2011, Japan's Fukushima Daiichi nuclear complex, suddenly underwent a series of highly radioactive explosions, meltdowns and melt-throughs, which continue on to this day. Japanese investigative journalist Yoichi Shimatsu believes that this disaster has seriously impacted and may even have caused the sudden breach in the Earth's protective ozone layer. (*Mainichi,* Japan, October, 3, 2011). Mr. Shimatsu offers a simplified explanation of chemical reactions in our upper atmosphere which have impacted this new Arctic ozone hole. A cold winter in 2010 /2011 generated dense stratospheric clouds over the Arctic region. These extreme temperatures and presence of moisture enhanced chemical reactions with a number of gases which deplete ozone. Fukushima's damaged reactors and burning fuel rods released tons of iodine, which is a highly-reactive ozone attacking agent. This ongoing disaster also released xenon, which quickly transformed into xenon-fluoride. Soon thereafter, our planetary Jetstream carried these newly formed xenon-fluoride compounds northeasterly across the Arctic Circle, looping back down over Greenland, Scandinavia and Russia. This, Mr. Shimatsu maintains, accounts for the oblong shape and direction of the recently expanded ozone hole. Since conditions leading to this unusually rapid ozone depletion are ongoing, it stands to reason that further depletion will continue. If any of this information is valid, we need to acknowledge and prepare for our new reality of ongoing, irreversible climate change... and then conscientiously prepare for what may soon become a very different world.

Enantiodromia

"Idealistic reformers are dangerous because their idealism has no roots in love, but is simply a hysterical and unbalanced rage for order amidst their own chaos." (William Irwin Thompson)

"Ideology paves the way for atrocity"
(Terrance McKenna)

A colleague sent me a You Tube video now going viral: *Anonymous: Bankers Are the Problem: The Root of All Evil"*. This message is delivered in solemn tones by a voice-disguised speaker wearing a Guy Fawkes mask, which has become the familiar icon of a leaderless movement known as *Anonymous*. If you skipped the course in British History, Guy Fawkes was a 17th century anarchist executed after his attempt to blow up Parliament. This mask, however, was popularized by the 2006 movie, *V for Vendetta*, which takes place in some dystopian future. The movie's main character known only as V, is a shadowy revolutionary freedom fighter who seeks vengeance upon fascist oppressors. In the *Anonymous* video the speaker advocates a need for "frontier justice" and for people taking the law into their own hands. If this wasn't alarming enough, he then refers to tragically oblivious Bourbon monarchs, Louis XVI and Marie Antoinette who lost their heads to the guillotine following the French Revolution of 1789. Anyone following Wall Street Protests spreading throughout the country can see that a meme for rebellion is in the air. One can also detect a growing support for "The Second American Revolution". Scattered throughout the New York crowds at *Occupy Wall Street*, one could actually hear calls such as "off with their heads". On October 4, 2011, *People Like Us* web site carried an article entitled, "Wall Street – Off With Their Heads" featuring the image of a guillotine. Readers were referred to a recent RT (Russian Television) interview with comedienne & activist Roseanne Bar who says that she favors a return of the guillotine. According to Roseanne, if corporations are "people" as the

U.S. Supreme Court recently ruled, then they should be tried for murder, fraud, larceny and other mayhem, and summarily beheaded. Here one can hope only that she exaggerates in order to make a point, and still her rhetoric invokes a disturbing historical precedent.

So far, tens of thousands who have taken to media outlets and the streets to protest the "economic royalists", have remained peaceful. Should the ruling classes and their minions overreact with extreme and violent suppression, tensions are likely to escalate with bloodshed on both sides. Since both language and images from the French Revolution have been evoked in the early stages of this confrontation, it might be useful to review the dynamics of that historical event where the guillotine became a symbol of the revolutionary cause.

A violent populist uprising in 1789, which began as a food riot (Let them eat cake) led to the overthrow of the clueless Bourbon monarchy.

After much public debate and deliberation, the king, queen and several other royals were eventually beheaded in 1792. This was followed by a period of violence and chaos that became known as "The Reign of Terror" (1793-94). Mass public executions were carried out as untold thousands of aristocrats and other "enemies of the revolution" lost their heads under the blade of the National Razor. Next in this cycle of horror, came executions of those who had both supported the revolution and carried out *The Terror.*

It has been said that few who initiate revolution actually survive that which they have set into motion. Nightmares of *The Terror* soon gave way to the rise of Emperor Napoleon, who was eventually overthrown in favor of a restoration of the Bourbon monarchy. Full circle! This dynamic has many names. The Ancient Greeks described this as a principle of *enantiodromia,* whereby that which is extreme has a tendency to morph into its opposite. Other versions advise that "you become what you resist", or "what you resist, persists" and "you become what you hate". Swiss psychiatrist C.G. Jung held that a superabundance of any force will eventually produce its opposite. This, he believed to be equivalent to the principle of equilibrium in the natural world. Any extreme, therefore, will be opposed by a systemic need to restore balance. At this point, it seems somewhat early to be able to forecast the outcome of our nation-wide protests which seem likely to become global. Nevertheless, we can be sure that extremes on either side will, sooner or later, morph into their opposite.

November 2011

The Reward of Patience

"Patience is a minor form of despair, disguised as a virtue"
(Ambrose Bierce)

As I seem to remember, it was St. Augustine who said something like... "The reward of patience is... patience". After four days of delay and two cancelled flights, I eventually arrived at my destination in Buenos Aires. Intermittent eruptions of a volcano in Southeastern Chile's Puyehue Cordon Calle chain, ongoing since June 4th, continue to create havoc for air travel to and within several neighboring countries. After a second cancellation my airline at Dallas-Fort Worth suggested an alternate flight to Chile and then to try again with a flight that approaches Argentina from another direction. On this flight to Santiago, a woman across the aisle from me inquired as to why I was traveling to Chile. I explained that this detour was necessary due to volcanic ash from Puyehue disrupting flights to Argentina. I was quite surprised when she reacted with annoyance and a facile smile to this rather straightforward information. She then informed me that this was not possible because "there are no volcanoes in Argentina", and besides, she lived in Cordova, Argentina and had heard nothing whatsoever about volcanic ash disrupting air travel. Although she was carrying an iPad, my observation that she could readily check this information was waved away as she quickly returned to her novel. I saw her again, only in passing, at Santiago airport as she was rushing around in distress since her flight to Cordova had been canceled, due to volcanic ash. While one can ignore reality, one cannot always ignore the consequences of ignoring reality.

My flight to Buenos Aires took off on time and I arrived four days later than my intended arrival date and grateful to finally be "home". After a short rest I took off again for another flight back across the Andes to Mendoza. Fortunately, flights to and from Mendoza were operating that day, although their air was heavily smogged with ashes coating the landscape and everything in it. Many residents and visitors were experiencing respiratory problems. This beautiful city situated at the foot of a great mountain chain is a favorite spot for tourism. Mendoza is located in the largest wine producing area of Latin America and also famed for its production of very fine olive oil.

The organizers that requested a trauma seminar there hadn't specified any particular theme. In such cases I just work with whatever comes up "in the field". Over time I have learned that what comes up in the field often has something to do with the history of a specific place where the seminars are held. This seminar in Mendoza was no exception. Based on the criteria of easy access, and a large modern auditorium with good acoustics, the organizing staff had arranged for our seminar to be held in a spacious building which is now a school. On our first day I began with my usual introduction and overview of individual and social trauma, including the importance of the "history of place". Soon thereafter, one participant revealed that this school had been a children's hospital and that she had been a patient there. Others soon followed with their stories of being patients there and having lost siblings who died in that very hospital. It also turned out that other participants had children who had died in that building. Child loss and medical trauma became a dominant focus of our two days in that facility. While these are difficult issues, I felt that the atmosphere was oppressive for some other reason. At the time, I attributed this feeling to the fact that our weather was unseasonably hot, windless and heavy with ash. On the third day our seminar was re-located to the headquarters of the local geological society. As we began, the group noticed that our atmosphere was decidedly lighter. Someone then informed us that the school, which was formerly a hospital, where we had been during the previous two days, also serves as the county morgue; which holds many abandoned and unclaimed bodies. And, not so surprisingly, since we were now located at a geological society, the massive disruptions of Puyehue arose as a topic.

Soon afterward I arrived in Santiago de Chile, this time for a scheduled seminar, and another volcano, Hudson was erupting. Volcanic eruptions in southern Chile usually don't affect air quality in Santiago because their wind patterns move in other directions. Clear skies also meant that my flight back to the U.S.A. could proceed without delay. Delay, however seemed to be a travel theme for this trip as I soon realized when arriving at a city that claims to host "America's friendliest airport". Supposedly in the interest of health and safety, robotic public service announcements encourage travelers to wash their hands frequently and make use of hand sanitizer gels available in all rest room facilities. After a cramped and sleepless, over-long flight, stiff as a B movie zombie, I nevertheless managed to find my way through the usual haze of airport banalities and locate the airport security line. The first TSA agent politely requested that I present my palms as he dusted both hands for traces of explosives. This seemingly innocuous swab test was positive. While calling for two female officers, he kindly explained that my culprit was probably hand sanitizer, body lotion or some kind of cosmetic or hair product. In time, two uber-authoritarian female agents, twice my size, took immediate charge and swiftly escorted me into a small grey windowless room. Behind closed doors, they explained that they were going to search through all belongings and perform a thorough pat down. In turn I also explained that I was not willing to go through their whole body backscatter x-ray machine, due to concerns about radiation exposure. My concerns are not unfounded given that these potentially carcinogenic devices have been banned from European airports due to health and safety concerns for both passengers and screening personnel. Declining their scanner, the agents said, made no difference whatsoever. Even if I agreed to go through their x-ray device they would still perform their thoroughly invasive pat down procedures.

Numb with fatigue, I silently contemplated the four, blank, featureless walls of our Orwellian enclosure while they carried out their pat down and searched through my travel gear for explosives. After much discussion between themselves, the two reluctantly concluded that the likely culprit was indeed hand sanitizer gel. Nearly an hour later, I was finally released with barely enough time to make it through the terminal to my connecting flight. What, one wonders, is the point of airport advisories encouraging passengers to make use of those ubiquitous hand sanitizers which will also trigger their explosive detectors? How many travelers are totally free of cosmetics, lotions, hair products known to trigger TSA's detection devices? While some might speculate that this is yet another tactic in TSA's malefic obedience training for sheeple, others just point to a juddering behemoth of a bureaucracy where one (sanitized) hand has no idea what the other is doing.

Nevertheless, throughout this mixed-message outrage, despite seething levels of cortisol, I was at least able to feign patience since that seemed to be my best option at the time. No surprise that a recent Congressional report calls Transportation Security Administration a "bloated and ineffective bureaucracy" and to that I would add "unnecessarily proto-military, adversarial and invasive". According to John Mica, R-Fla., chairman of the House Transportation and Infrastructure Committee, "TSA has lost its way...It's time for reform". Any such action could be a long time coming, if ever, from our legislature which, bowing to the food lobby, recently declared pizza to be a vegetable. Small wonder that the millions taking to our streets are running out of patience.

First They Ignore You...

"There's class warfare all right, but it's my class, the rich class, that is making war, and we're winning" (Warren Buffet)

Recent developments in the ongoing Occupy Wall Street Movement have brought the timeless wisdom of Mohandas Gandhi to mind: "First they ignore you, then they laugh at you, then they fight you, and then you win". Events here and now in our 21st century are moving in a much more rapid progression than was the case during Gandhi's days of social protest and non-violent revolution. The trajectory so far has been true to his template, in that these protests were ignored by main stream media outlets for over three weeks before nationwide coverage slowly began. And then, as coverage opened up, most of the shallow talking heads initially feigned ignorance as to what this populist fuss was all about. Slowly however, the message of the OWS movement continued to gain traction through social media, twitter and alternative information sources. No longer able to ignore, mainstream coverage initially split along party lines. Mass media corporate holograms, denizens of the ruling One Percent, launched an all-out campaign to ridicule and discredit protesters as unwashed hippies, over-educated college types, homeless street criminals, domestic terrorists and so on. Our alterative media however, took up the OWS cause and deflected some of the derisive humor back at the one-percenters. This caught fire in viral videos on You Tube and on late night comedy and talk shows. Repressive regimes have limited defenses against political satire and other forms of truth revealing humor. As a result, our government, military and police who protect self-serving, elite members of the top One Percent, have inevitably resorted to unimaginative episodes of brutal suppression; involving various forms of violence and attempts at overt and covert intimidation.

As of now, it appears that the OWS movement is finding itself somewhere out in an open, and as yet unknown, field of opportunity and challenge. This very young and vulnerable movement must now navigate a precarious path between derision, laughter and fight. So far, protesters have done an impressive job of getting their message out to anyone who might be at least somewhat willing to listen. American citizens have, finally and somewhat belatedly, opened their eyes to the fact that crime and government policy have become interchangeable. Vast numbers of people have given up on their elected representatives and taken to the streets, barricades, parks and plazas. From all walks of life, these are patriotic citizens who have finally realized that positive change is not going to come from above. Their protest began in the Wall Street district, which they consider to be a symbolic target of populist discontent, with wide-spread and ongoing abuses by arrogant financial oligarchs.

Millions have now awakened to the reality of services cut, wrecked neighborhoods, a soaring income gap, illegal foreclosures, and sudden tuition hikes. Something finally clicked here in a country which prides itself on promoting an egalitarian society. Family incomes are declining while profits of the rich and super-rich, especially those in finance, politics and war profiteering continue to soar. ("Let them eat cake"). Those who study history know that too much wealth in the hands of too few sets up a volatile dynamic. In a time of catastrophic levels of unemployment, unions crushed, demolished regulation, unaffordable health care, decline in services, intrusive surveillance, erosion of civil liberties, overt racism, and a growing resentment of Wall Street's control of both parties; civil unrest is inevitable. In view of the many recent, violent, suppressive responses that legitimate protesters are now facing; they have an imminent and crucial choice. Their decision as to whether to meet violence with escalating violence or remain on a non-violent path, will likely determine the outcome which could lead to peaceful social change or yet another cycle of violence.

Victims and Perpetrators: Murakami in Spain

"I can bear any pain as long as it has meaning"
(Haruki Murakami, 1Q84)

The processing of collective trauma has been an important theme throughout the work of Japanese writer and translator Haruki Murakami. A literary superstar in his own country he is now considered to be one of the world's greatest novelists. In 1995 Japan suffered two major social trauma events. In January there was a devastating earthquake in Murakami's hometown of Kobe. Then in June, a terrorist attack by the *Aum Shinrikyo* religious cult released deadly Sarin gas into the Tokyo subway. This event led to Murakami's first non-fiction project: *Underground: The Tokyo Gas Attack and the Japanese Psyche* (2001), comprised of essays and interviews with both perpetrators and victims. Two years later he published, *After the Quake*, a collection of mesmerizing stories about those whose lives were profoundly shaken by aftershocks of personal and social upheaval. This volume includes a personal favorite, the heartbreakingly weird short story, "Superfrog Saves Tokyo".

In June of this year, during a speech in Barcelona on the occasion of accepting the International Catalunya Literary Prize, Murakami spoke about the recent tsunami and nuclear disasters in northeastern Japan. The author expressed his belief that the Japanese people should have rejected nuclear power after having learned through the suffering of *hibukasha* (atomic survivors) just how badly radiation leaves scars on the world as well as the well-being of humanity. While donating the financial proceeds from his prize to victims of the March earthquake, tsunami and nuclear crisis, he offered the following:

As you know, the Japanese people are the only people in history to experience the blast of an atomic bomb. In August of 1945 atomic bombs were dropped on the cities of Hiroshima and Nagasaki from United States bombers. Over two hundred thousand people lost their lives. Almost all of the dead were unarmed civilians. But my purpose today is not to debate the pros and cons of those acts. What I want to talk about is not only the deaths of those two hundred thousand people who died immediately after the bombing, but also the deaths over a period of time of the many who survived the bombings, those who suffered illnesses caused by exposure to radiation. We have learned from the sacrifices of those people how destructive a nuclear weapon can be, and how deep the scars are that radiation leaves behind in the world, in the bodies of people. There is a monument set up to pacify the spirits of those who lost their lives to the atomic bomb at Hiroshima. These are the words engraved there: Please rest in peace. We will not repeat this mistake.

This is an historic experience for us Japanese; our second massive nuclear disaster. But this time no one dropped a bomb on us. We set the stage, we committed the crime with our own hands, we are destroying our own lands, and we are destroying our own lives... While we are victims, we are also perpetrators. We must fix our eyes on this fact. If we fail to do so, we will inevitably repeat the same mistake again somewhere else." (Translated by Emanuel Pastreich in, *Circle and Squares*, July 18, 2011).

December 2011

Trickle-Down Tyranny

"Apparently, conspiracy stuff is now shorthand for unspeakable truth. (Gore Vidal)

In a recent article for *Natural News*, "Adopting Tactics of Tyrants" (November 22, 2011), Mike Adams gave name to a cultural miasm that I have been observing with increasing discomfort. In view of stories such as, "food Nazis" raiding farm picnics and ordering everyone to destroy their food; nursing home staffers in Atlanta waterboarding an 89 year old dementia patient using techniques borrowed from Guantanamo Bay; and routine sexual and other harassment of air travelers by TSA goons. Arrest of young children is becoming commonplace, as is use of lethal Tasers by militarized police; against the deaf, wheelchair-bound, elderly, pregnant women, mentally ill and anyone else who does not immediately "comply". The news media for this past month of November was filled with images of jut-jawed law, bullyboy enforcers of a corrupt authoritarian order. We watch in horror as uniformed members of the NYPD casually pepper-spray, toxic, concentrated mist directly into the faces of non-violent protesters; as though these innocent people were some sort of non-human insects. No surprise therefore that a competitive shopper thought it justified to pepper spray 20 other consumer-addicted customers in order to "get an upper hand" in the race for a Black Friday sales day bargain. Just as children mimic the actions of their parents, people are following examples set by "the authorities". By the way, Pepper Spray, made from rocket fuel, contains trichloroethylene, toxic to anyone within range and may cause permanent visual impairment.

Trickle-down tyranny is not uncommon in totalitarian societies. People who are bullied, bully others because they can; it's within their job description or they were "only following orders". Those who enjoy inflicting pain, suffering, and power over others, under cover of the law and freedom from accountability, will always thrive in an authoritarian atmosphere. *In Death in Life: Survivors of Hiroshima*, Psychiatrist Robert Jay Lifton identified another aspect of this dynamic. In his study of post-war Japanese reaction to the atomic bomb, he found that many did not blame the USA for dropping it on their cities. Instead they chose to believe that America must be a very great power to have such a weapon. These Japanese managed their fear by choosing to identify with the aggressor and the bomb, and then sought nuclear power for themselves. Coping with fear by identifying with the aggressor could also explain some of what is going on in our country now. And then there is the old adage that "you become what you resist". In this so called "war on terror", Americans have taken to terrorizing each other in the name of patriotism. Omnipresent messages from Big Sis and Homeland Security encourage us to adapt an attitude of suspicion and spy on our fellow citizens as potential "domestic terrorists"... "If you see something, say something". Alert citizens who value their remaining freedoms would do well to also say what they see while monitoring the actions of our "authorities". This information needs to be shared through any and all available mainstream or alternative media outlets, internet posting, cell phone cameras and twitter. In a truly democratic society this message of "see something, say something" can and should work both ways.

Winter Solstice: Darkness and Not Knowing

"The night spins a fine membrane like the film inside an eggshell" (Roxana Robinson)

"There are two ways of spreading light, to be the candle or mirror that reflects it" (Edith Wharton)

My mother's family is Cornish, and many old Celtic traditions survived in some form or another in our holiday celebrations. Cornwall is located in Southwest England just below Wales, and their mid-winter festivities include the burning of the Yule Log. This remnant of ancient fire festivals marks a passing of the old and advent of the new. At the darkest point in the year a new log was brought to a hearth and burned along with scraps from the previous year's burning. This practice is to insure the continuity of protection and prosperity from one year to the next and also down through subsequent generations. While I don't remember any Yule logs being burned in our fireplace, a decorative facsimile, flanked by candles and sprigs of evergreen, always appeared on our dining room table throughout the holiday season. More recently, we have enjoyed a confectionary version in the form of a *Buche de Noel*, a cylindrical cake covered with chocolate frosting, sugary holly leaves, berries and tiny marzipan mushrooms. While most Celtic winter festivals are heartening, Solstice is also observed as a serious time of darkness and not knowing.

Solstice, from the Latin "sun stands still", marks our shortest day of the year here in the Northern Hemisphere. On or about December 22nd our sun appears to stand still in the sky in that its noon time elevation does not appear to change from one day to the next. This time of stillness and long dark night is also revered as a time for turning inward. Focus now on being rather than doing, while awaiting the return of the light.

In the archetypal realm I have found the image of the Hanged Man in the Tarot, to be an interesting representation of this time of year and also of both psychological and spiritual states. Swiss psychiatrist C.G. Jung believed that this mysterious deck of cards, of unknown origin, reflects archetypal images and profound patterns in humanity's collective unconscious. On the collective level, one could speculate as to reasons why this graphic image could prove timely for the American Empire at the end of 2011 as well as the overall future of mankind and the planet. Dr. Jung saw the Tarot as a means to traverse dark and light distances between the collective unconscious and the awake and aware conscious mind. In *Jung and Tarot: An Archetypal Journey*, Sallie Nichols takes an in-depth look at multiple meanings encoded within the Hanged Man as the twelfth card in the deck's Major Arcana. She prefers the Marseilles Deck since it is one of the oldest designs available today. In her view, this twelfth card represents "suspense" as well stagnation, frustration and some forms of depression.

A single upside down figure appears suspended between the poles of two trees above a crevasse which could also be a deep abyss. Both hands are bound behind his back and he hangs there helplessly tethered by a rope around his left foot. In other versions the Hanged Man is depicted with coins, as symbols of worldly values, tumbling from his pockets as he dangles between the polarities of known old and unknown new. This custom of reverse hanging has been called "baffling", a word used nowadays as synonymous with thwart, frustrate or confuse. The practice is also a traditional punishment for "traitors". As history reveals, anyone whose individual conscience is in opposition to a prevailing paradigm can appear disloyal to the establishment. Often such individuals find themselves "upside-down" in relation to friends, family, government and other Powers That Be. Life as a valued citizen is at risk of suspension. Saul Bellow explored this theme in his novel, *The Dangling Man*. Individuals, groups and entire nations can encounter a time of trials during which one stage of existence may suddenly or gradually come to an end. They then find themselves feeling helpless and "hung up" by their circumstances. Feeling utterly up-ended, and suspended between known and unknown, and disconnected from our roots, is a very familiar element in the human condition. This twelfth card offers a possibility that at such times the best and maybe only option is to be still; wait, hope and pray.

Referring to this experience as a psychological state Jung wrote, "The patient must be alone if he is to find out what it is that supports him when he can no longer support himself. Only this experience can give him an indestructible foundation." In this regard, Nichols believes that the Hanged Man, and potentially "everyman" is supported by Nature's tree which connects him with the sturdiness of his own inner nature.

The potential that this experience can result in something transformative, appears in the way that the position of his legs form the numeral four. This symbolic number indicates that completion and solidarity are taking form deep within his unconscious. This archetypal formation implies that the Hanged Man also has an access to grace, as he acquires a new understanding and possibly acceptance of that which he cannot change. Major Arcana XII also marks the linear time limits of human reality within our twelve hours of day and night and our yearly count of twelve months. I found a resonant image in the Nordic rune *Isa* or Ice, which is depicted as a single vertical line. As a variation on themes of stillness and suspense, Isa heralds both the frozen state of winter and the winter of spiritual life. This rune speaks to those who find themselves in situations to which they are essentially blinded by some level of white-out. During such times, one may be powerless to do anything except submit, surrender and even sacrifice some long cherished desire. "Be patient" is the wisdom, for this is a fallow time that precedes re-birth. Shed, release, cleanse away the old. This will bring on a thaw. Be still, for what you are experiencing is not necessarily the result of your actions, but of conditions of the time, against which you can do nothing. Exercise caution in your isolation and do not persist in attempting to impose your will. Remain mindful that a seed of unrealized potential is present in the shell of the old. Trust your own process and watch for signs of spring. (Ralph Blum, *The Book of Runes*, 1983, St. Martin's Press, NYC)

This suspended image of the Hanged Man stays with me as we are on the cusp of what promises to become an iconic year of 2012. No doubt the viral meme about the end of the Mayan calendar has added to an atmosphere of both anticipation and dread. The truth is that we live in a time of darkness and not knowing; but also of a mass media hologram of hype and disinformation. The Mayan calendar is nowhere near its end. In the coming year, I will not be looking to the skies for the Messiah, Twelfth Inman, sword-bearing Jesus arriving on a fiery cloud, extinction level asteroids, comets or solar kill-shots. Most likely, over the course of this coming year, we can expect that new people will be born, others will die and we will adapt.

January 2012

Mayan Mystery Solved?

"You don't want to listen to academics all the time...Professor X and Dr. Y may be very, very impressive people with their credentials, but they have prejudices and fixed views of the past which they are going to stick to, come what may.
(Graham Hancock)

One of the ongoing questions in Pre-Colombian studies is what happened to the Ancient Classic Maya, after a sudden collapse of their civilization which had reached its height between 300 and 900 A.D.? While indigenous Maya still reside in various parts of Mexico and Central America, some 15 million of their ancestors seem to have abandoned most of their cities and quite suddenly disappeared. Various speculations about this mass disappearance include climate change, deforestation, famine, overpopulation, collapse of trade routes, epidemics, ongoing wars between city states, foreign invaders, a top heavy elite, and volcanic eruptions. From a modern perspective it seems reasonable to postulate that this massive social trauma resulted from some combination of known and unknown, man-made and natural catastrophes. Some scholars believe that most of the Maya population from that era either died out or migrated to other regions. A few New Agers have suggested that the Ancient Maya disappeared into a parallel dimension or even took off with Sky God benefactors for some other galaxy. Nevertheless, the Mayan enigma remains timely for this New Year of 2012 given a renewed interest in cycles of fractal time encoded within the Mayan calendar.

Toward the end of 2011 I was surprised to come upon an article with the title "1,100-year old Mayan ruins found in North Georgia. At first glance this piece by David Ferguson appeared to be a hoax. This startling information, published here and not in an in an archeological journal, was accompanied by an image of the "Aztec calendar" which is actually not a calendar. While the Aztec took over most of their calendar from the Maya, the two are not identical and the erroneous image accompanying this article is of the Aztec Sun Stone which was actually an altar used for human sacrifice. Now, to return to the subject of Pre-Columbian calendars. The most important difference between the Aztec and Mayan time keeping systems lies in the fact that the Aztecs did not include the Mayan long count; a fugue-like chrono-vision which has been a source for a flurry of recent speculation. It is generally believed that the Mayan long count began in 3,114 BC and the current cycle will end on December 21, 2012. However, it is important to understand that this 25,920 year cycle is not even close to an end of the Mayan calendar, which continues on into much further units of time.

Despite an erroneous image of the Mayan calendar, Ferguson's article piqued my curiosity because if true, this would be one of the most important archeological discoveries of modern times. His source, I soon discovered, was an article by Richard Thornton, *Architectural and Design Examiner*, December 21, 2011, who has also written a new book, *Itsapa: The Itza Maya in North America*, (January 2012). Thornton recounts activities and findings of University of Georgia's Mark Williams. According to Thornton, Williams, a highly respected specialist in American Southeastern archeology, has been excavating the Kenimer Mound site in the mountains of North Georgia, believed to be at least 1,100 years old. Ruins there appear to be the remains of a city built by Maya who fled north in order to escape a variety of inhospitable conditions. Thornton maintains that Williams began by leading an expedition to explore this Kenimer Mound, which turned out to be a large five sided step pyramid dating from about 900 A.D.; built by methods common to Central American Maya. The earliest maps of this area show the name Isate, which is what the Itza Maya called themselves. Only Itza Maya and the ancestors of Creek Indians in Georgia built five sided step pyramids in the Americas and there are dozens of such structures in Central America.

A Cherokee village near the mound was named Itsa-ye, translated into English it means "place of the Itza (Maya)".

The Kenimer Mound project was joined by South African archaeologist Johannes Loubser whose firm dug two test pits under stone structures to obtain soil samples which registered radiocarbon dates of 1000 A.D. Loubser also uncovered pottery shards made from around 770-850 A.D. believed by some to be consistent with the time of the Classic Mayan diaspora. Pottery found at the Ocmulgee National Monument (900 A.D.) in central Georgia appears to be virtually identical to Maya Plain Red pottery made by tribal commoners. This could suggest that Maya who emigrated northward to the American Southeast were common folk who then became elite to local indigenous cultures and eventually blended into Creek, Cherokee and various other tribes. If this is true, then the fate of the Maya elite and ruling classes still remains unknown. At this point, all speculations around this topic have remained controversial. Professor Mark Williams dismisses Thornton's article referring to William's excavations as "bunk"; Professor Louber says that his findings were interpreted out of context. Further challenges are in the offing from a group of Southeastern Archeologists who doubt the theories of a Northern diaspora undertaken by the Maya after a period of collapse.

You Become What You Resist...

"If you don't have a plan, you become part of somebody else's plan."
(Terrance McKenna)

Variations on this theme frequently appear in individual and social trauma work and in ordinary daily life, as well. While these phrases differ, their message is quite similar: What you resist, persists, you will become what you hate, extremes tend to morph into their opposites, (*enantiondromia*), victims and perpetrators are likely to exchange roles, and so forth. A recent example appears in Robert C. Koeler's article "The Spiritual Jackpot" (December 15, 2011) in *Commondreams.org.* Koeler was disturbed by a *NY TIMES* opinion page entry by Ojibwa author David Truer, "How Do You Prove You're an Indian?" In essence, his story recounts how billions in casino profits have led to a process of tribal disenrollment. There was a time, Truer says, when each tribe had their own way of determining who was a member, usually based upon language, residence and culture. Nowadays, casino-rich tribes who have adopted Western values of sacred profit, are casting out lifelong members so that monetary gains can be distributed among fewer recipients. This is very consistent with contemporary American capitalistic practice, which seeks to concentrate wealth in as few hands as possible.

Over the past decades, California tribes have dis-enrolled something like 2,500 people with allegations of a lack of proof of authentic bloodline ancestry in that particular tribe. Within such actions, Koeler detects another silent consequence of Western genocide from previous centuries, when many tiny tribes were decimated and later reconstituted. As a consequence of this and other factors, many full blooded Indians are descended from more than one tribe. As casino tribe disenfranchisements continue, many members are finding themselves and their families denied their heritage and sometimes forced, together with their children, out of their homes. Ironically, many victims of disenrollment policies have had to turn to the U.S. government by asking Congress to empower the Bureau of Indian Affairs to provide legal recourse.

Japan: Diaspora Underway

"No amount of radiation is safe. Every dose is an overdose. (George Wald, Nobel Laureate, 1953)

According to *Yomiuri Shinbun* (January 5, 2012), the Japanese government/industrial complex has plans underway to build new "Small Japan" in a southern Indian township of Chennai that will house some 50,000 residents. Their new city is to include "Japanese-quality" infrastructure, seaside resort, industrial park, hospital, shopping mall and golf course. Industrial plants housed in this new region are expected to be operational by 2013. And indeed, the *Times of India* (January 11, 2012) has reported that the Tamil Nadu government has signed a memorandum of understanding for location and construction of this new 1,500 acre "Japan Town". "It's all about money" said Dr.

Haruki Madarame, of Japan's Nuclear Safety Commission, whether "it" is about a nuclear power plant, nuclear waste facility or Japanese-only city in southern India. Critics have likened this project to a post-apocalyptic, post-nuclear reality with a safe haven community only for the select from government and industry. Elderly, infirm and especially radioactive *hibakusha* (outcasts) will find no place there. Japanese society has a long history of stigmatizing and shunning anyone contaminated with radiation. Other less elitist efforts of evacuation are being covered online by Iori Mochizuki's, *Fukushima Diary,* which lists addresses and web sites from the international community willing to assist Japanese, their families and loved ones in the challenging process of finding new homes. If you wish to help or know of people or organizations willing to be of assistance, the contact information is available at "Evacuate": http://fukushima-diary.com.

February 2012

Compassion Fatigue: Another Form of Heart Disease

"When you've learned your lessons, the pain goes away" (Elizabeth Kubler-Ross)

Here in the USA February is our traditional "Heart Month". Amongst Valentines, roses, ribbons, chocolates and advice about cardiac health, it may also be time to shed some light on another form of "heart disease". What used to be called "burnout", now has many labels including: compassion fatigue, soldier's heart, ongoing-overwhelm, secondary or vicarious traumatization and nervous exhaustion. This phenomenon, which now has countless cross–cultural variations, presents a serious and sometimes life threatening challenge to personal and professional caregivers. Over time, some find themselves at risk of becoming "just too tired to care". We can recognize compassion fatigue in a pattern of sudden or gradual disengagement; emotions are blunted, relationships fail, acute or cumulative exhaustion affects motivation, drive and often physical health and well-being. Frankfurt born psychoanalyst Herbert J. Freudenberger was the first to name this syndrome. The Oxford English Dictionary credits him with first use of the term "burnout" in 1974. Whatever the label, this phenomenon is painfully real. People in the healing and helping professions; doctors, nurses, teachers, rescue and social workers and yes, even clergy, can fall prey to this insidious form of emotional exhaustion. In such a state one feels helpless, hopeless, negative and even cynical; about oneself, work, life and the overall state of the world. Germans have a very precise word for "feeling the pain of the world" which they describe as "*Weltschmertz.*"

Trauma specialists are not immune to the pitfalls of compassion fatigue, since we come in constant contact with the darker aspects of the human condition. Compassion fatigue can have a social dimension as well, and is a contributing factor to an ability to walk on past increasing numbers of homeless veterans, mentally ill and other unfortunate citizens living out on our streets. Barely into 2012, I am already sensing something like "Apocalypse Fatigue" in response to the media blitz about the Mayan calendar, Armageddon, fright-wing politicians, The Rapture and other end of the world predictions. This has given rise to a rash of cynical bumper stickers such as, "After the Rapture Can I Have Your Car?" Mainstream media reports are filled with war casualties, atrocities, terrorist attacks, false-flags and violent revolutions. We are also facing economic collapse, political scandals, climate change, earthquakes, volcanic eruptions, solar flares and possible pandemics. Even worse, an ongoing meltdown of three nuclear reactors in the Fukushima Daiichi Complex is poisoning air, food and water throughout our biosphere. I could go on, but this might understandably result in your tuning out your already tragedy-overdosed sensibilities. Small wonder that some people need to deny and minimize the catastrophic. Others deal with overwhelm by shunning headlines and ignoring the news in favor of shopping, sports and celebrity gossip. Confronted with overwhelming suffering, our violence-numbed nervous systems may seek to self-regulate through distraction, recoil, and shutdown. When something, or seemingly everything, is just too much, time is needed for relief and self-regulation. San Francisco satirist Mark Morford suggests that a clear grasp of our current situation calls for "ice cold sake and a nice warm bath". This is one option, admittedly not available to all, and there are others.

It is important to remember that we are not as powerless as it may seem and that we do have options. One of the hallmarks of a maxed-out and traumatized state is to lose the perception of options. When a sense of option is restored, one is able to move toward balance. There is much wisdom in that old saying, "You can't change the world". We do, however, have an option of changing our response to that which we cannot change. We also have an option to take time to examine, to what degree a clash between expectations and reality is adding to and perpetuating distress. There are clear indications that we are now in a period of profound meteorological, geologic and socio-economic upheaval, which is likely to continue for an indefinite period of time. In view of this reality, it would be wise to anticipate and prepare for enormous waves of change. We would do well to focus on a necessity for adaptation and resiliency. If the big picture seems to be daunting, we can resolve to stay informed and then conserve energy and attention for the needs of our own immediate lives; the families, loved ones and communities to which we belong.

Wislawa Szymborska

February is also my birthday month, which arrives this year on the cusp of the seventh decade of a long and eventful life. I found a poem for this occasion which resonates on many levels.

ABC.

I'll never find out now
What A thought of me.
If B ever forgave me in the end.
Why C pretended everything was fine.
What part D played in E's silence.
What F had been expecting, if anything.
Why G forgot when she knew perfectly well.
What H had to hide.
If my being around meant anything
to J and K and the rest of the alphabet.

This was written by Polish poet Wislawa Szymborska (1923-2012) who won the Nobel Prize for Literature in 1996. She died in her home in Krakow at the age of eighty-eight. An anthology of her work has been translated into

English by Stanislaw Baranczak and Clare Cavanagh as: *View with a Grain of Sand. ABC* was first published in a December issue of *The New Yorker,* in 2004 and caught the attention of Dana Stevens, ("The Poem Above My Desk", *www.slate.com*, 2012/02/03), who was drawn to the simplicity and complexity within a play of alphabet letters as a wistful meditation on the infinite and unresolved stories within each of our lives. Upon hearing of the poet's passing, Katha Pollitt wrote " ...Szymborska's signature quality is the way she puts tragedy and comedy, the unique and the banal, the big and the little, the remembering and the forgetting, right next to each other and shows us that this is what life is; as we see in, *The End and The Beginning:*

After every war someone has to tidy up.
Things won't pick themselves up, after all.
Someone has to shove the rubble to the roadsides
so the carts loaded with corpses can get by.

Szymborska's most serious themes of history and its many horrors; the passage of time and love and loss, often co-exist with a wry ironic twist. She lived through appalling occupations by the Nazis and then decades of Soviet, Stalinist communism. After a short "socialist-realist" phase of her youth, she withdrew any interest in grand political schemes in favor of irony, wit and the individual. For Szymborska, it is the one who matters; transient, blind, foolish - plaything of chance - still also urgent, insistent and full of his own meaning - alive. (Katha Pollitt: http://www.*thenation*.com)

March
2012

Rush to Judgment

"Feminism was established to allow unattractive women easier access to the mainstream"
(Rush Limbaugh)

Just in time for International Women's Day, American radio shock-jock Rush Limbaugh set off a firestorm of protest in response to his latest misogynistic rant against "feminazis". The fact that Limbaugh is a controversial buffoon is not really news, but this time this self-styled "hatriot" may have gone too far ....much too far. After Georgetown law student Sandra Fluke was denied an opportunity to testify before an all-male, Republican congressional committee, convened to discuss whether contraception should be included in women's health care coverage, she received an invitation from the Democrats. Ms. Fluke's testimony included the reality that these expensive contraceptive medications are valuable and necessary for many reasons including treatment of gynecological disorders such as ovarian cysts, and endometriosis. Mr. Limbaugh promptly responded by slandering Ms. Fluke as a prostitute and slut who would accept government money for the purpose of having sex. He railed on, that since this makes Sandra a prostitute, therefore in return, she should repay taxpayers by posting her sex videos on line so that we can all watch. If that wasn't toxic enough, he characterized this sincere young woman as a greedy nymphomaniac whose parents should be ashamed. There was quite a bit more of this vile rhetoric which has gone viral on the internet. Limbaugh's rant then served to provoke internet postings of familiar anecdotes about this much married, childless, radio host's obesity, prescription drug addiction, fondness for Viagra and 54 million dollar a year salary.

While there have been calls to remove Rush Limbaugh from the airwaves, this will not solve the problem. From a systemic perspective,

Limbaugh is not the problem, but rather the symptom of a problem which is larger than one media personality. Consider the reality that his top-rated "angry white guy", paleo-conservative, show, boasts tens of millions of listeners who apparently share and support his blatantly misogynistic values. He has complained of the presence of "lard-ass women in politics" and boasts a belief that "women are basically cats that can walk"

(SadyDoyle, http://inthesetimes.com, 4/8/2012).

Overblown Limbaugh also serves as an ongoing spokesman for Christian, right-wing, sexual fundamentalists who equate contraception with promiscuity. These mostly Republican folk are drawn to punitive absolutes and promote faith based abstinence programs as the only acceptable solution to unwanted pregnancy. While Limbaugh's initial response to the outrage provoked by his sexist rant, was to find it all "absolutely hilarious", his tune soon changed as commercial sponsors began leaving in droves.

He then scrambled to issue a half-hearted, fingers crossed, apology in hopes of staving off at least some financial backlash. One long time sponsor has made it clear that they are sticking with Rush; our American military.

Limbaugh's programs are broadcast world-wide over taxpayer supported *Armed Forces Network,* owned and operated by our Department of Defense. It seems that they share similar values given that over 30% of women in our military report sexual assaults by commanding officers and fellow service members. Many of these assaults remain unreported for reasons that are not difficult to imagine. *VoteVets,* a coalition of Iraq and Afghanistan veterans, has released a letter from female veterans requesting *Armed Forces Network* to drop Limbaugh's show from its programming. In part, their letter reads:

"Our entire military depends on troops respecting each other – women and men. There simply can be no place on military airwaves of sentiments that would undermine that respect. When many of our female troops use birth control, for Limbaugh to say that they are "sluts" and "prostitutes" is beyond the pale. It isn't just disrespectful to our women serving our country, but it's language that goes against everything that makes our military work. Again, we swore to uphold our Constitution, including the freedom of speech, and would not take that away from anyone – even Limbaugh. But that does not mean the *AFN* should broadcast him. In fact, it shouldn't."

Pentagon spokesman George Little responded with a statement that our military network will continue to air Rush Limbaugh and is "unaware of any plans to review that decision". (Faiz Shakir, http://*thinkprogress.org*/2012/03/05).

Nepenthe

"The only journey is within". (Rainer Maria Rilke)

When I lived in California, the Big Sur coast was a favorite destination for rest and renewal. These nature oriented restorative visits always included some time at *Nepenthe*, a family owned restaurant and café established in 1949. Indoors or out this is a lovely place where one can contemplate a spectacular coastline along and above this stretch of the Pacific. Their outdoor terrace features an open fire pit and a driftwood sculpture of a phoenix rising from a circular bed of flaming orange torch lilies. *Nepenthe*, derived from the Greek, (no+grief) is the name of a mythical drug of forgetfulness believed to have originated in Egypt. As the story goes, the wife of mythical King Thonis gave this potion to Helen, daughter of Jove to induce forgetfulness and surcease from sorrow. Homer mentions this amnesiac in *The Odyssey,* and it appears again in Poe's, *"The Raven"*: *Quaff oh quaff this kind Nepenthe, and forget the lost Lenore"*.

Grief is a normal human response to loss and usually resolves over time. When it doesn't, loss often involves unresolved trauma, as well. Forgetfulness is not the solution. This view, however, is not shared by pharmaceutical and other companies actively pursuing development of amnesiac drugs or other mind control techniques for treatment of trauma. Any such protocol only serves to perpetuate a mechanistic and outdated Cartesian illusion that human beings are biological machines in need of fixing. The big fallacy here is that erasing painful memories will heal trauma because trauma is only in the mind or located in some specific area of the brain. While this is partially true, it is also true that trauma is a psycho-somatic experience. The body remembers. For more about this reality see Peter Levine's books, tapes and web site: http://www.traumahealing.com, and neurologist and psychiatrist Robert Scaer's, *The Body Bears the Burden.*

Amnesiac treatments would set up a situation where the body remembers something that the mind does not and this can create panic attacks and other serious disturbances. The downside of memory erasure as a solution to emotional problems was recently given a light hearted treatment in the zany romantic comedy, *The Eternal Sunshine of the Spotless Mind.* Nevertheless, ethical problems involved with any such procedure are very serious indeed. Among those wary of memory altering drugs we find *The President's Council on Bioethics,* an advisory group of physicians and scholars formed in 2001. In their report, this council expressed concern that dampening painful memories, or erasing them altogether might disconnect a person from the reality of their true selves. More about this viewpoint is available in Scott LaFee's, "Blanks for the Memories".
(www.*cognitiveliberty*.org/02/11/2012.)

Among the major consequences of trauma are dissociation and a profound sense of alienation. These "broken connections" represent a fragmentation within the self, in relation to others, and a larger environmental matrix supportive of human life. Memory erasure by chemical or other means, risks further fragmentation in an already fragmented psyche. This atomistic, seriously disconnected, view of human suffering has little to offer a suffering soul's need for re-connection and wholeness. From my perspective, an essential goal of trauma work is to find ways to expand and include, and then become larger than whatever has happened to us. It has been my experience that trauma is not something that can be "fixed" or that one can really "get over". Overwhelming life experiences are integral to who we are and who we will become.

Beware the Bucky Balls

"We've arranged a global civilization in which most crucial elements profoundly depend on science and technology. We have also arranged things so that almost no one understands science and technology. This is a prescription for disaster...sooner or later this combustible mixture of ignorance and power is going to blow up in our faces."
(Carl Sagan)

On this one year anniversary of six reactors being damaged at Fukushima Daiichi complex, three of which are in ongoing meltdown, this crisis has not resolved. Early on, physics Professor Michio Kaku warned, "Meltdown is forever". As our entire biosphere is being contaminated with radioactive isotopes in our air, food and water, information crucial to public health has been minimized, distorted and withheld by corporate controlled international media outlets. Their reasons all add up to some all too familiar variation of, "we don't want to create panic". Therefore and necessarily, most of the accurate and useful information has been taken up by the alternative media and its blogosphere. From Japan one finds valuable postings at http://*fukushima-diary*.com and here in the USA, *Rense Radio* has provided ongoing, in-depth coverage including frequent interviews with environmental reporters Yoichi Shimatsu in Asia and Michael Collins in California : http://www.enviroreporter.com.

We are learning more on a daily basis and the news is not good. With various half-lives, the following are some of the radioactive components of the venomous vapors spewing forth from Fukushima Daaichi Complex; Iodine 131 (8 days), Cesium 137 (30 years), Strontium 90 (29 years), Plutonium 239 (24,000 years) and Uranium 235 (700 million years). And it gets worse. A January 27, 2012 University of California (Davis) report, "Uranyl-peroxide enhanced nuclear fuel corrosion in seawater", spells out a heretofore unseen danger. This Fukushima nuclear accident brought together compromised irradiated fuel and large amounts of seawater in a high radiation field.

"Based on newly acquired thermochemical data for a series of uranyl-peroxide compounds containing charge-balancing alkali cations, we show that nanoscale cage clusters containing as many as 60 uranyl ions, bonded through peroxide and hydroxide bridges, are likely to form in fuel and become thermodynamically stable and kinesthetically persistent in the absence of peroxide. And, they can potentially transport over long distances."

This report was a joint project of U.C. Davis, *Sandia National Laboratories* Department of Civil Engineering and Geological Sciences, and The University of Notre Dame Department of Chemistry and Biochemistry, published January 23, 2012 (*Proceedings of the National Academy of Science, Journal*).

These nanoscale cage clusters, of Buckminsterfullerenes are also known as "bucky-balls", due to their spherical shape, with multiple flat sides similar to the trademark geodesic domes designed by the inventor and futurist, Buckminster Fuller. Radioactive bucky-balls were formed as seawater was poured over the molten cores of the damaged reactors, turning water into peroxide and creating bucky-ball broth. Although uranium is heavier than water, uranyl filled, fused-ring bucky-balls are lighter and more mobile in water. Thus, they are able to quickly transport Fukushima contaminated ocean water all along the Pacific Rim and infuse the entire marine food chain. These hot particles are virtually indestructible; they radiate and are potentially carcinogenic if inhaled. Ocean borne bucky-balls are also transported through the winds, sea spray and mists, which can be carried as far as 300 km inland. The discovery of these silent killing bucky-balls carries dire implications for all 44 nations of the Pacific Rim. At present, the U.S. Environmental Protection Agency and National Oceanic & Atmospheric Administration are not testing for Fukushima melt-down radiation.

April
2012

Columbine Re-Visited

"The use of direct force is such a poor solution to any problem; it is generally applied by small children and great nations." (David Friedman)

On April 20, 1999 Eric Harris and Dylan Klebold opened fire with guns and bombs in their Littleton, Colorado, High School cafeteria during peak lunch hour. Despite the presence of two armed security personnel, the boys were able to move into the library, where they killed 12 students and a teacher, and wounded 23 others before the homicidal pair turned their weapons back on themselves.

At that time, I was living nearby and I began what was to become a decade long inquiry into many facets of this tragedy. I later published my findings in, *A Question of Balance: A Systemic Approach to Understanding and Resolving*

Trauma, in a chapter entitled "War in Colorado" and another as "Aftermath". One fact that drew my immediate attention was that according to their diaries, these Neo-Nazi teens described their homicidal plans as a "military operation", and their focus was upon bombs more than guns. Their original plan was to initiate a mass scale bombing to blow up their school and then blow up rescue workers as they arrived on the scene. In addition to military assault rifles, their homemade arsenal included more than 48 carbon dioxide bombs, 27 pipe bombs, 11 one and a half gallon propane containers, 7 incendiary devices with 40 plus gallons of flammable liquid, hand grenades, and two duffle bag bombs with 20 pound petroleum tanks. Only after their homemade bombs failed to detonate did they resort to guns.

As of 2012, the community of Littleton has not healed, and for some people many important questions remain unanswered. Further events and more revelations about the killers and their families continue to shift the focus in a still evolving collage of social trauma with deep roots in unresolved wars, racism, terrorism, and genocide. Added to that are gun control laws, psychiatric medications, media disinformation, and hype. In a tragedy that involves this much complexity, a cause is neither obvious nor linear. Nevertheless, in one sense at least, Eric and Dylan's "military operation" has succeeded in fostering the safety and security measures leading to an increasing militarization of our schools. Public schools are coming to resemble military and prison facilities with an increasing presence of security apparatus; check points, metal detectors, mobile surveillance cameras, chain link fences, police on campus, surprise and even strip searches for students. We can now expect naked body scanners as part of the prom night experience and more and more elementary and pre-school school students handcuffed, taken away in police cars and charged with "felony offences".

If you think that I'm exaggerating, take some time to read the daily news; or better still, check the policies of your local school district.

Chernobyl 2012

April is the cruelest month, breeding
Memory and desire, stirring
Dull roots with spring rain,
Winter kept us warm, covering
Earth in forgetful snow...
(T.S. Eliot, The Burial of the Dead)

This month marks the 26th anniversary of the nuclear disaster at the Chernobyl Nuclear Power station in Ukraine when it was still part of the former USSR. Until Fukushima, this unforeseen catastrophe was the worst industrial accident in history. And the danger is far from over. A hastily constructed concrete sarcophagus designed to entomb the damaged reactor is seriously deteriorating, and radiation continues to leak into the surrounding environment. Speaking in 2000, former UN Secretary General Kofi Annan warned, "Chernobyl is a word we would all like to erase from memory. But, more than 7 million of our fellow human beings do not have the luxury of forgetting. They are still suffering every day...their exact numbers will never be known." (AP 2000). Explosions from Chernobyl's reactor unit number 4, released a series of radionuclides high into our atmosphere and these plumes contained 400 times more radiation than the bombing of Hiroshima. During the last days of spring and the beginning of summer these potentially lethal plumes fell over hundreds of millions of the unaware. Carried aloft by a Jetstream highly charged with seeds of fire; silent, odorless, invisible, radioactive, hot-particles drifted over 40% of Europe and Scandinavia, as well as territories in Asia; including Turkey, Georgia, Armenia, Emirates, and China. Also North Africa and North America. The immediate and most concentrated fallout descended upon Ukraine, western Russia and Belarus. An unusually intense round of forest fires in the course of the following summer served to further spread these dangerously hot-particles.

Early attempts to ascertain and evaluate the consequences to human health and the environment were made especially difficult due to cover-ups and an overall Soviet policy of political secrecy. In April of 2011, journalist John Vidal published an account of his visit to the still highly contaminated areas of Ukraine and Belarus. As a result, Vidal challenged any clueless pundit downplaying the risks of radiation to talk to doctors, scientists, mothers, children and villagers who have been left with the consequences of a major nuclear accident:

"It was grim. We went from hospital to hospital and from one contaminated village to another. We found deformed and genetically mutated babies in the wards, pitifully sick children in homes, adolescents with stunted growth and dwarf torsos, fetuses without thighs or fingers and villagers who told us that every member of their family was sick...20 years after the accident and one still sees many unusual clusters of people with rare bone cancers. Villagers testified that a "Chernobyl Necklace" (thyroid cancer) was so common as to have become unremarkable. ("Nuclear's Green Cheerleaders Forget Chernobyl at our Peril" *Guardian*.co.uk, April 1, 2011)."

Having visited Russia and worked in a trauma clinic there during the aftermath of the Chernobyl explosion and meltdown, I have also seen these horrors. And, I would second John Vidal's challenge to any who carelessly promote those smooth, corporate-controlled media lies of "safe, clean, nuclear energy". How many glib proponents of "nuclear safety" are willing to confront reality in documentaries such as "*Children of Chernobyl*", widely available on Youtube.com. While radiation is especially dangerous to the unborn and young, other long-term effects have been noted in the form of accelerated aging, decline in mental function, gastro-intestinal disorders, type two diabetes, immune suppression, ocular changes, auditory disorders, endocrine diseases, reproductive cancers, diseases of the blood-forming organs and the circulatory system. Mental health specialists in contaminated areas of Ukraine, Belarus and Russia report an all-pervasive sense of depression and "victim mentality" in these populations. We are fortunate that the largest and most complete collection of data, concerning the negative consequences of the Chernobyl accident on the health of people and the environment, is now available online: Alexey V.Yablokov, et. al:

http://www.strahlentelev.de/yablokov%20Cher nobyl%20book.pdf

Anyone willing to read the results of Yablokov's definitive study will see that nuclear power plants carry exactly the same, if not greater, risks to all living things as nuclear weapons. Given the nature of the nuclear power industry and its close ties to the military (nuclear weapons), media and academia; so-called free societies must consider the necessity for independent monitoring of radiation in our air, food and water and that the results be made freely available to the public. Activists have also recommended independent monitoring of the health of all children born and living within a 50 mile radius of any nuclear facility.

Public access to information about the dangers of radiation and the options for minimizing exposure is especially important now in the wake of the March 11, 2011 Fukushima Daiichi disaster. Chernobyl occurred in a land locked, relatively isolated region and only one reactor burned for just 10 days. Fukushima, however, happened along the coast of a densely populated country. In the Daiichi reactor complex, six reactors were severely damaged, three in total meltdown. All six nuclear facilities have been leaking and spewing deadly radioactive particles into the air, food and water of our entire Northern Hemisphere; with no end in sight. Mainstream media outlets are mostly silent, and target populations in North America and elsewhere remain, for the most part, unaware.

May
2012

British Falklands vs. Argentine Malvinas

"Maybe we should ask the Falklanders how they feel about a war"
(Lord Francis Pym, British Foreign Secretary)

Now that increasing tensions are once again surrounding these islands we find an all too familiar, post-war story in journalist Tom Clifford's, "Suicides Outpace Combat Deaths, and Benefits Access a Struggle for Veterans of Falklands/Malvinas War."
(http://truth-out.org/4/14/2012).

I have some vague memories of this distant war which began on April 2, 1982 as it was briefly covered in the USA. Our decidedly pro-Anglo coverage took the tone of a comic-opera conflict with photo ops of handsome, warrior Prince Andrew flying a search and rescue helicopter over the South Atlantic. His nephew, handsome warrior Prince William is currently in the Falklands on a similar assignment, although there are no overt combat operations at this time. And, there is still some hope of peaceful resolution.

Until I began working with combat trauma in Argentina and also the UK, I was unaware of the seriousness of this tragic event for soldiers and their families; on both sides of this brutal exchange. Conflict over the sovereignty of the Falkland/Malvinas, South Georgia and South Sandwich Isles, as British Protectorates, began with an Argentine invasion force under orders from the military dictatorship known as the Junta. These soldiers were mostly young, untrained conscripts who were initially proud to be called upon to serve a patriotic cause. Most believed that they would only represent a kind of occupation force and then this conflict would be sorted out by some diplomatic process. Many of these young men had never ventured beyond their remote and rural farms, towns and villages, and some had never seen snow. As they landed upon ice-cold island shores, it became immediately apparent that they were totally unprepared. Dressed in sandals and other inadequate clothing, conscripts would be soon freezing in the trenches and grappling with sub-standard equipment that they had no idea how to use. After much bloodshed, the humiliated Argentines surrendered to the well-trained British forces on June 14, 1982. Although this war was short, it continues to kill veterans from both countries. In Argentina I learned that 649 soldiers died in active service and at least 400 traumatized others took their own lives. Accurate statistics are difficult to come by since many of these suicides were covered up as accidents or illness, due to the religious condemnation and social shame associated with these acts. Entire communities have lost nearly all of their young men to this conflict.

Veterans and their families call this "a forgotten war", since few want to remember this painful episode. On the British side, 255 soldiers died on active duty while a startling 264 veterans have taken their own lives. While survival guilt may have been a major factor, as is the case with many post-war suicides, another form of guilt may have contributed to these deaths. During a visit to the UK, I had the opportunity to speak with veterans of the Falkland's War who expressed little satisfaction in their victory. As professional soldiers, they were expecting "a real fight". Many of their Argentine opponents turned out to be ill equipped farm boys and "instead of a fight, there was a massacre". Many British troops were ashamed of the slaughter. This British victory was a political boost for Margaret Thatcher's conservative party. The repressive dictatorship of the Military Junta was subsequently removed from power and Argentina returned to democratic government in 1983. One might wonder why two great nations would continue to risk further trauma and bloodshed over ownership of these remote windblown islands. Argentina claims that they are battling some last vestiges of colonialism while the British insist that they are defending the citizens of their protectorate. While both may be true, it is also a fact that this region of the South Atlantic is very rich in natural gas and oil.

Japanese Diaspora: Update

"Fukushima's nuclear disaster is a nightmare. Ghostly releases of radioactivity haunt the Japanese countryside. Lives, once safe, are now beset by an ineffable scourge promising vile illness and death. (Paul Zimmerman, A Primer in the Art of Deception).

Known and unknown perils of radiation continue to increase throughout the Japanese archipelago. An elevated, leaking, seriously wobbling spent fuel pool above Fukushima Daiichi reactor 4, tilts and teeters on the verge of collapse in a highly active seismic zone adjacent to the ocean. Nuclear expert Arnie Gundersen warns of a "Chernobyl on Steroids" if this spent fuel pool ignites into a potentially unending radiological fire. In a recent interview with Pat Thurston, the usually temperate Gundersen addressed the situation at severely damaged reactor four. He cautions that if this spent fuel pool should go dry or collapse, the result would unleash radiation equivalent to 800 nuclear bombs. In this case, he advises those who wish to survive to immediately relocate south of the equator. www.enenews.com, (5/04/2012).

Given the real possibility of this extinction level event, Tokyo and other densely populated areas may need to be suddenly and permanently evacuated, as was the case with the Chernobyl meltdown disaster in the former USSR.

This unfortunate information raises the question of how and where to re-locate over forty million people. In my January 2012 blog I reported that the Japanese government/industrial complex plans to build a new Japan Town in Southern India designed to accommodate 50,000 upscale residents. This Japanese-only facility is intended for the still healthy elite and elderly. Infirm and radioactive *hibakusha* (outcasts) are not included in this design. Therefore, some other plan is urgently needed for millions of others who may need to leave with some hope of surviving further contamination. Apparently, there are talks ongoing with both Russia and China as to possible strategies for massive relocations. Discussions with Russian officials are reported to be focusing on the disputed Kuril Islands located in their Oblast region. Located approximately 810 miles northeast from Hokkaido Japan, these 56 islands stretch all the way out to Kamchatka; separating the Sea of Okhotsk from the North Pacific. Soviet Forces captured the Kurils from Imperial Japan during the final days of World War II. And now, the current Japanese government argues that their return is critical given that their people are in desperate need of a place for massive resettlement. There are also reports that Japan is considering an offer by China to relocate tens of millions of Japanese people to their mainland, uninhabited, "Ghost Cities" constructed and abandoned for unknown reasons. Satellite images reveal sprawling cities built in remote parts of China. Architecturally complex public buildings, plazas and other open spaces are mostly unused and some estimate the number of empty homes at 64 million.

If this Japanese diaspora should become a reality, it would become the largest human migration since the 1930's when Stalin's forced deportations sent tens of millions to re-settle Russia's remote far eastern regions. While this current crisis may seem to be a problem only for Japan, it could also happen here. At present we have 31 GE Mark I and Mark II boiling water reactors within the United States; exactly the same models that GE/TEPCO constructed in Fukushima. For more specific information see: (Brad Jacobson, "The Worst Yet to Come? Why Nuclear Experts Are Calling Fukushima a Ticking Time Bomb", May 4, 2012).

Why has the public not heard more about this ongoing and potentially increasingly lethal disaster? GE is heavily invested in nuclear power industries and weapons production and also partnered with Tepco. GE also owns and controls most of our mainstream media outlets... and with those facts in mind, it is not so difficult to connect the dots.

Global Trauma:
Contemporary Issues

"The real battle in the world today is not among civilizations or cultures but among the different evolutionary futures that are possible for us and our species right now." (C. Otto Scharmer, Theory U: Leading from the Future as it Emerges)

Every once in a while I Google myself to see what information is available on the web about my conference presentations, books, blogs, and seminars about trauma; as well as social and global trauma in general. These internet searches sometimes produce unexpected results. In The Netherlands for example, I discovered that I am known as "The Grand Old Dame of Social Trauma Work"

(I hope this sounds better in Dutch). And just recently I came up with an item on a Norwegian web site, that Peter Levine and I wrote as part of a series of columns we did for *The Redstone Review* when we were living in Colorado:

(www.hellinger.no). Our monthly column was entitled "Contemporary Issues and Their Effects of Social Trauma" and from that collection "Asteroid Threat" appeared on the Norwegian site. This piece was written before 9/11 and after Chernobyl but the true extent of that nuclear disaster was not yet established. At that time, as we approached the millennium, there was some media attention devoted to a growing awareness of our planet's vulnerability to the consequences of a comet or asteroid collision. While these outer space objects are still a threat, a more immediate source for an extinction level event is now present in the triple meltdowns and ongoing radiation emitted from six damaged reactors at the Fukushima Daiichi Complex. Now in 2012, threats falling from the sky have more to do with radiation in the Jetstream than asteroids or comet collisions.

Nevertheless, in re-reading this decade-old column I realized that my views concerning any number of massive global trauma events have remained somewhat consistent. In response to the question: How to orient toward a possibility of an extinction level event, I would again offer the following: "Violence and destruction are integral to the nature of the Universe, present at every level of existence; elemental, geological, organic and human. For those of us who have encountered the violent side of human nature, it seems important to develop a perspective on forces of change that are larger than good and evil or 'us and them'. While we humans do seem to have some control over our lives, we can also seem to be powerless beings, subject to an unfamiliar order. While the majority of global trauma is taking place on a scale vastly beyond human awareness, we can still find some reassurance in the notion that the forces of life seem to be more than equal to the forces of destruction. Those whose lives have included encounters with forces of darkness and destruction may find some solace in compassion for what might be called 'impermanence', as well as compassion for all passing things. Realizing that we exist in a difficult time of perceivable loss and gain has the potential to open our imagination beyond this moment, and to travel to realms of a much larger story. (Anngwyn St. Just and Peter Levine, 1999)

None So Blind

"None so blind as those who will not see." (Matthew Henry, 1662-1714)

Hundreds of *Alaska Air Lines* flight attendants are reportedly suffering from mysterious rashes, itchy skin lesions and hair falling out. The cause is said to be their new 100 percent polyester uniforms. The problem with this reasoning is that these uniforms were issued in 2011, and the Alaskan wild life suffering from these same symptoms, do not wear uniforms. Polar bears, walruses, otters and seals are losing their fur and strange lesions have also been found on many of these mammals. As far as I know, only Glen Canady of, *Before it's News,* has been willing to speculate that these flight attendants and the northern wild life are suffering from early signs of radiation poisoning coming over in the jet stream and ocean currents from the ongoing Fukushima Daiichi nuclear disaster. ("Are *Alaskan Airlines* Flight Attendants Getting Sick from Fukushima?" http://beforeitsnews.com, 5/14/2012).

And then, we also have the mysterious deaths of some 900 dolphins and thousands of sea birds along the Peruvian coast on up to their border with Ecuador. The dolphins suffered from multiple skin lesions and the maritime birds were thought to have starved because they could neither swim nor fly. The reasons given for this wildlife debacle range from climate change and dragnet fishing, to oil shore drilling, the acoustic effects of military undersea sonar activities, and as yet unidentified viral mutations. Renowned biologist Guillermo Boigorrea from the University of Trujillo said that scientists were also analyzing the sea water. "It's unbelievable that the Oceanic Institute has still not given a reason for the massive death of pelicans and dolphins. I believe that we are trying to protect certain interests".

The Peruvian health ministry has urged the public to stay away from the beaches near Lima and along the northern coast until the cause of the die-off is known. (5/14/2012)

This already disturbing news was soon followed by reports of 2000 coastal birds found dead along the coast of central Chile. Officials there put the blame on fishermen's nets, and environmentalists suspect oil exploration activity. While any or all of these explanations may have merit, no one has considered the possibility that the common factor in flight attendant's illnesses from the polar north on down to Peru and Chile, has anything to do with radiation. This is especially interesting given the high levels of radiation found both in Japanese seaweed and kelp forests all along the coast of California. (Michael Collins, *enviroreporter*.com)

The unfortunate fact is that massive quantities of radioactive materials and contaminated water from Fukushima Daaichi's spent fuel pools continue to flow into the Humboldt Current, familiar to the Japanese as *Kuroshio*. Also known as the Black Stream, the *Kuroshio*/Humboldt is the driving force for the North Pacific current. This relatively narrow, rapidly moving band of water is conveying a concentration of radioactive poisons around the North Pacific; across the Bering Strait to southern Alaska, Canada and the West Coasts of the United States and Mexico. When this contaminated North Pacific Current arrives along the continental shelf, it divides.

One stream veers northward along the coasts of Alaska and Canada and into the breeding grounds of seals, sea otters, and walruses (and the flight paths of *Alaska Airline* crews). The other stream turns south and becomes the California Current which divides again into the Equatorial Pacific; moving from Mexico to the Philippines where it rejoins the Humboldt and the Peruvian, heading south along the coast of South America. Mega-scale hydrodynamics reveal that Japan's nuclear disaster is in the process of contaminating most of the vital fisheries of the Pacific. (Yoichi Shimatsu. "The Death of the Pacific Ocean", December 2011).

Why a reluctance to connect the dots that lead toward radiation as a potential and ongoing threat in all of these so-called mysterious air and sea events? From a psychological perspective, denial can be understood as a protective defense mechanism when there are insufficient resources needed in order to face an overwhelming reality. While denial can be protective, head in the sand is a structurally vulnerable posture which can also lead to disaster. As always, there are also issues of power and greed. It is the nature of governments and industries to withhold information "in the public interest", in order "to avoid panic", and to place profit and social control above public health and safety. If the truth about the ongoing, massive, radioactive contamination of the entire Pacific Ocean were to be widely acknowledged, this would have a devastating effect on fishing industries, tourism and air travel, which would soon reverberate throughout the economic food chain. And, there will always be those who just do not want to know. But like gravity, radioactive contamination in air, food and water, which is increasingly dangerous to all living things, is here whether you believe in it or not.

Trauma: Time, Space and Fractals

"For people like us, who believe in physics, know that the distinction between past, present and future is only a stubbornly persistent illusion" (Albert Einstein)

Fractals have been called "the fingerprints of God".....and my newest book, *Trauma: Time, Space and Fractals: A Systemic Perspective on Individual, Social and Global Trauma*, explores the role of fractal time in an ongoing effort to understand the causes, experience and healing of many levels of trauma. Physicists such as Roger Penrose are now telling us that the Universe, and time itself, is composed of an infinite series of expanding and contracting cycles within cycles. This new version of reality conjures images of vast cosmic cycles, mirrored in smaller cycles; such as human civilizations, communities and family systems, planetary cycles, and in the rhythms of our individual lives. Each of our lives is lived as an integral fragment within other cycles, which are nested within increasingly larger cycles. These larger cycles also contain smaller cycles and still smaller cycles because they contain universal fractal patterns which repeat themselves in non-linear self-similar ways, as described in the axiom "As above, so below". In many traditions, if not all, these hidden designs are recognized as fate.

The paperback English language version is now available: Anngwyn St. Just, *"Trauma: Time, Space and Fractals* at Amazon.com along with generous endorsements from Drs. John Bilorusky and Peter Levine.

A Spanish translation by Gloria Davila is available from Alma Lepik in Buenos Aires, Argentina.

June
2012

What to Believe?

Nuclear power is a hell of a way to boil water.
(Albert Einstein)

On the morning of June 7, 2012, I logged onto the web site of my favorite weather man who calls himself Dutch Since. His Website is at: (www.sincedutch.wordpress.com).

He was startled to find a posting of extremely high radiation levels recorded by three different monitoring systems in the upper Mid-West. I was immediately concerned for a number of reasons, including the fact that I have close family members living in that region. While radiation levels vary throughout our country, any counts per minute over 100 is cause for serious concern and these unprecedented levels were as high as 7,074 cpm. Online *Radiation Network* responded by turning off their monitors and *Black Cat Systems* issued a statement claiming malfunction. This story could have ended there, except that RSOE EDIS, The *Hungarian Association of Radio Distress Signaling and Info-communications* (hisz.rsoe.hu) which operates an Emergency and Disaster Information Service, reported a nuclear event in exactly the same area where the radiation spikes appeared. Later in the day, multiple mainstream news outlets carried a story that operators of the Davis-Besse Nuclear Power Station in Oak Harbor (near Toledo), Ohio, revealed that they had discovered and then contained a "pinhole-size leak spraying radioactive coolant". This, they claim, was contained by their collection system and radiation never got outside of the plant into the surrounding atmosphere. Operators also claim "no injuries" along with the time worn, all too familiar, "no danger to the public", that we have been hearing since the advent of nuclear testing programs. Are we to believe that a pinhole–size, contained leak had nothing to do with sky high and potentially lethal radiation spikes in that exact same location? Some people are willing to believe almost anything rather than pursue or even face a difficult truth.

While the corporate controlled mainstream media stuck to their pin-hole story, on June 8, 2012, Anthony Gucciardi offered a more credible version of the Ohio events: "Nuclear Cover-Up: Explosions Filmed Near Blacked Out Radiation Zone": (http://*naturalsociety*.com).

He reports that eyewitnesses near the elevated radiation zone are now sending a large number of photos and videos documenting massive explosions accompanied by unmarked helicopters, A-10 Thunderbolts, military personnel and a hazmat fleet from the Department of Homeland Security. Witnesses also reported "explosions everywhere...seriously consistent, loud booms lasting an hour or more". It was rapidly becoming apparent that tall tales of pinhole leaks and malfunctioning monitors were no longer sufficient to cover events of this magnitude. Yet another story would now be needed. So again on June 8th Gucciardi came out with the latest spin: "Breaking: Major Base Running 'Containment Exercise' Amid Censored Radiation Spikes" http://naturalsociety.com.

This new version of events claims that Minot Air Force Base in North Dakota is running a nuclear containment exercise; hence a need for media black-out and military hardware. This version is less than reassuring since our military usually announces their exercises well in advance in order to avoid alarming the public. At the very least, what we see here is a highly organized level of non-disclosure enabled by complicit mainstream media outlets.

A worst case scenario presents us with a possibility of yet another highly dangerous nuclear event seriously endangering public health and welfare. With loved ones living within an hour of the Davis-Besse Nuclear Power Station, I decided to look into the 34 year history of this facility. According to *Wikipedia* and other sources, Davis-Besse has a highly dubious safety record with many incidents, violations and criminal prosecutions of personnel convicted of intentionally misleading federal regulators as to the dangers of this plant. More information is available in *Union of Concerned Scientists Report on Davis-Besse.*

Those who still believe in that "safe, clean, green energy" fairytale, offered by nuclear power proponents, are welcome to go back to sleep. The awake and aware, will heed the handwriting scrawled upon the deserted walls of Chernobyl. We cannot afford to ignore the disastrous partial meltdown at Three Mile Island, present horrors of Fukushima Daaichi, recent nuclear events at Missouri's flooded Fort Calhoun nuclear facilty, California's San Onofre and now Davis-Besse. And, there may well be other nuclear events of which we are, as yet, unaware. Our most reliable information now comes from alternative media and the foreign press. The internet provides a rich source of information about the dangers of radiation and options for defense, protection and minimizing exposure, on web sites such as www.rense.com and www.enenews.com (energy news) which offer an entire section of nuclear radiation news; as well as Michael Collins, www.enviroreporter.com and Army Major General Albert Stubblebine's information, www.healthfreedomusa.org

July 2012

Solar Flares and Human Health

"The Sun is new each day"   (Heraclitus)

On July 5th my husband and I noticed that we were both having an unusually awkward day, spilling things, knocking into familiar objects and feeling headachy, rather woozy, and "off" for no discernible reason. Then, when all of our telecommunications blacked out I remembered something about solar flares being predicted for this time frame. Later, when our internet connection returned, I decided to look into the phenomenon and the possible effects on human health. According to the staff at *Space Weather News,* an enormous, sprawling sunspot known as Active Region 1515, 100,000 kilometers long, and wider than 15 Earths set end to end, has spewed 12 M Class (moderately severe) solar flares since July 3rd. These flares occur when magnetic energy that has built up in our Sun's atmosphere is suddenly released along with electrons, protons, and heavy nuclei...resulting in a force ten million times greater than energy released from a volcanic explosion. These solar events have a potential to disrupt satellites, power grids and communication infrastructures.

According to a recent study published in the *New Scientist*, solar storms can also have an effect on the electromagnetic fields of Earth and of humans and other biological entities.

Columbia University psychiatrist Kelly Posner maintains that our pineal gland, which regulates circadian rhythm and melatonin production, is sensitive to magnetic fields. This circadian regulatory system is dependent upon repeated environmental cues to synchronize internal clocks. Dr. Posner further explains that magnetic fields may be one of several radiation hazards to humans, since intense solar flares release highly charged energy particles which can contaminate mammals in a manner similar to low-energy radiation from nuclear blasts. (Mitch Battros, www.earthchanges.com, 12/21/2011).

In a similar vein, TAO Grand Master Lim of the *Qi-Mag Institute* maintains that the extreme magnetic effects of strong solar flares can affect our human central nervous system, brain activity, balance, thought patterns, behavior and mental-emotional responses. Therefore, all living beings may experience some degree of nervousness, anxiety, worries and jitters. More sensitive people may experience short term memory loss, heart palpitations, headaches and become irritable, lethargic and exhausted. Electromagnetic blackouts may also disrupt medical devices such as cardiac pacemakers. It stands to reason that physically and emotionally stressed biological systems are the most vulnerable.

(Monique Muller, "Solar Flares and their Effect on Human Health", www.americanlivewire.com).

My husband and I are both feeling much clearer, however my 96 year old mother was not so fortunate. She was admitted to hospital on July 5th with cardiac fibrillations when her pacemaker malfunctioned. Her cardiologist believes that any association with recent solar flares is purely co-incidental. I am not so sure. In any event, it is a fact that we are now heading into a peak in our Sun's eleven year flare cycle with 2013 expected to bring about even more violent space weather events. Given increasing evidence that this Solar Cycle 24 is likely to seriously impact life on Earth, it seems clear that upcoming and ongoing flares should become an integral part of mainstream media radio and television weather forecasts. As it now stands, most of the important information is available only on the internet and alternative news outlets. Becoming aware of the potential of these flares to destabilize all biological organisms on a number of levels, would be especially wise given these stressful times of rapid change and geopolitical upheaval. An excellent authoritative exploration of this topic is available in Mitch Battros': *Solar Rain: The Earth Changes Have Begun*, (Earth Changes Press, 2005).

Birthing the Future®

"Birth is not only about making babies. Birth is about making mothers, strong competent capable mothers who trust themselves and know their inner strength." (Barbara Katz Rothman)

The health care system as we have known it, is in chaos, and this includes maternity care. This system and the mindset that created it are going through a painful and dysfunctional labor, struggling to stay in control. (Suzanne Arms).

My long-time colleague, film maker and fellow keyboard activist, Suzanne Arms has a new project. Her latest DVD, *"The Time is Now"*, the first volume in a global project, roundtable film series, includes important information about preventing trauma during the pregnancy, birthing process and delicate post-natal period.

For those unfamiliar with Suzanne's work, Obstetrician and Gynecologist Christiane Northrup, M.D. describes Suzanne's vision as a tapestry woven of knowledge from ancient and cross cultural wisdom to modern science; (cellular biology, neurobiology, psycho-immunology, and attachment theory) together with ecology, feminism and spirituality. Suzanne's seven books are based upon her belief that love, fear, peace and violence begin in the womb and this is where one finds our roots of either faith or alienation. As she describes her work: "I work at the beginning of life where patterns are set. We must transform how we bring human beings into the world and care for each childbearing woman and mother/baby pair from conception to the first birthday, when they are one biological system and the baby's developing brain and nervous system are laying down patterns for a lifetime."

Suzannes' insights are important for us all, for as she says, women's experiences and their feelings about themselves, their babies, and motherhood translate directly into the thoughts and biochemistry that lay down patterns in a human nervous system. These patterns shape how we see ourselves as children as well as the relationships that we form as adults and how we care for others and our world. How we treat women who bring children into our world, with either honor and tenderness, or neglect and abuse, profoundly influences the direction of local and global society.

Knightmare in Colorado

'Dark ...is an attitude, a mood, a view and a fashion statement. It hints at things that are better left unseen, of subterranean things, nefarious, anti-social things, underbellies and the underground, things proper society wishes to avoid. (Dana Stevens, Review of: The Dark Knight Rises, Slate Magazine, 2012)

"We're All in the Crosshairs"
(Randall Amster, New Clear Vision, July, 2012)

On the morning of July 21st, I awoke to news of a mass shooting incident at a theater complex in Aurora Colorado. At first glance the story described a gunman killing 12 and wounding at least 59 during a midnight showing of the new Batman movie, *The Dark Knight Rises*, at the Century 16 Theater Complex at the Town Center Mall. My first priority was to call my son, an avid fan of sci-fi and fantasy productions, who happens to live in that very neighborhood. Unlike many others with similar concerns, I was among the fortunate and greatly relieved when he answered his phone. An early riser, he had already heard the news and reminded me that there had been a number of death threats leveled at high profile reviewers who had been critical of this film. While my son and his wife were planning on seeing this movie, he said that they wouldn't have gone to that theater because the Town Center Mall had a history of problems. This is important because many locations of these large scale massacres have a violent "history of place".

Biologist Rupert Sheldrake, who has written about morphogenetic fields, also believes that places can have "fields of memory". This became clearly evident during my ten years of research into the nearby Columbine High School massacre and the ongoing and unresolved aftermath. Results of this extensive investigation were published in my second book, *A Question of Balance: A Systemic Approach to Understanding and Resolving Trauma.*

Gang activity surfaced at Town Hall Center, around the year 2000, along with accusations of racism and repressive security guards. One has to also consider the probability of much earlier violence in this area during tribal conflicts in the Arapahoe times, as well as atrocities following the arrival of the US Cavalry.

As this dreadful news of movie theater violence unfolded it was reported that a gunman clad in full body armor, tossed two gas canisters into the crowd and opened fire into a sold out midnight showing of the Batman movie premiere. Immediate casualties included 12 dead and at least 59 wounded and many unnamed others traumatized, as well. Witnesses reported that a masked assailant, carrying a variety of assault weapons, entered through a side door and began shooting during an action scene in the film, initially confusing people who thought that resulting pop-pop noises and aerosol fog might be part of the evening's entertainment. This surreal blend of onscreen and real time violence, added to a delayed response, with subsequent confusion and resulting panic. Other surreal elements in this event include the unfortunate fact that Warner

Brothers previewed this Blockbuster Batman Premier showing with a trailer from their upcoming *Gangster Squad,* which included scenes of a gunman shooting up people in a movie theater. Equally disturbing was the quote from *Newsweek's* assistant culture editor, Marlow Stern, predicting that "Dark Knight audiences will be blown away".

After completing his rampage, the shooter calmly exited the theater, surrendered to police and informed them that his apartment was booby trapped with explosive devices. Their suspect was identified as James Holmes, a 24 year old graduate student studying neuroscience at the nearby Anshutz Medical Campus (formerly Fitzsimmons Army Medical Center). Sporting a wild mop of carelessly dyed red-orange hair, he reportedly identified himself as The Joker. However, at this point, any specific relationship between the shooting and this movie is unknown. Since this event was a premiere, Holmes could not have seen the latest version of the Batman saga, and therefore, a more likely source of "inspiration", could be a 1986 comic book version of Dark Knight which shows a massacre in a movie theater.

Caution is needed here, since the initial information and simplistic speculation about causality and motive in the Columbine massacre; "trench coat mafia", bad parents, bullied outsiders and so on, eventually proved both misleading and untrue. Already, misinformation about the Holmes family has gone viral with stories about James' blueblood ancestors coming over on the Mayflower, ignoring the fact that he was adopted. Many questions remain unanswered for now about possible mental illness, psychotropic drugs and/or medication; eyewitness reports of a second shooter, an accomplice and of course, motive.

This gun related incident, like so many others in our recent history, has served to re-ignite all too familiar debates over gun control, with our usual advocates of the left, right and center repeating their equally inflexible positions. These then appear on our expected and all too predictable, seriously scripted, mainstream media outlets. And of course, our always interesting conspiracy theorists have joined in discussions throughout the alternative media with seriously considered suspicions of a staged event. According to their description, the Aurora massacre took place in a location known to be a hub of the military/industrial complex. Holmes was studying on a $26,000 dollar government research grant, and had a documented interest in subjects such as "temporal-spatial perceptions", possibly related to mind control. This in turn has prompted questions about the military ties of his psychiatrist and a possibility of mind control programming. For those unfamiliar with MK Ultra and other covert government projects involving mind control there is extensive information about these supposedly defunct experiments at: www.bibliotecapleyades.net/esp_cointelpro06.ht ml and a 1979 ABC News Special documentary is available on You Tube: "Mission Mind Control".

For those with this mind set, possible motives for setting up a Manchurian Candidate type of patsy would include a pretense for government seizure of private weapons or just another seemingly random event, set up to terrorize citizens into seeking more security through increased surveillance and suppression. All in all, it seems that the viewpoints all around are deeply entrenched. Further discussions, amiable or otherwise, are not likely to change minds that are already made up as to what did or did not happen in that Colorado multiplex theater. As film critic Roger Ebert said, "We have seen this movie before". Yes, and with our opposing political lines so firmly drawn, we are likely to suffer through many, or even an endless Knightmare of ongoing reruns.

From a systemic perspective, gun control might address the symptom but would not resolve our underlying dysfunction. In his recent article,

"We're all in the Crosshairs", Randall Amster takes a deeper look at the complexities underlying this veritable shooting gallery/abbatoir, within which we now find ourselves. He postulates that this kind of recent violence is a not unexpected response to a society that places alienation, dependency and casual brutality at its cultural core. Any serious change would require us to be willing to ask really hard questions about this culture of violence that we ourselves have created. Amster maintains that the mass-shooting phenomenon that happens routinely here in the USA is part and parcel of a society that legitimizes force, medicalizes despondency, individualizes burdens and demonizes dissent. Such a system has many people feeling utterly trapped, isolated and powerless to effect change; and some are likely to act out their desperation in horrifying ways. He goes on to ask, to how many violent images is an American child exposed? How many marketing campaigns exploit feelings of diminished self-esteem and alienation? How do the mind numbing drones of mass media glorify the use of force, often on a daily basis? How many toxins, chemicals, and other alterants infuse our skies, our food and water supply and contaminate the larger environment? In how many ways are we made to accept dehumanization in our economic arrangements, as we inhabit a world in which everything is for sale and anything/anyone can be bought for a price?

Ours is an anti-life society where nothing is guaranteed, not our military might, not our civil liberties, not our privacy and certainly not a midnight movie in the suburbs. It just might be that if we were willing to stop arguing long enough to honestly face our situation that a positive shift could begin toward a direction of health. We could choose to begin an authentic engagement that takes nothing and no one for granted, prioritizes systemic health and individual potential; as well as one that moves from lethal rigidity that serves the rich and powerful, to favor of one that acknowledges the dignity of all human beings as well as an urgent need to behave responsibly in our local and global environment.

http://truth-out/org/7/29/2012.

Yes, it is late, and our odds are slim, but it could just be that we still might have something like a choice.

Update: Following a suicide attempt James Holmes reportedly told a fellow inmate that "an evil therapist programed him to kill".

August 2012

Oak Creek, Wisconsin: Our New Normal

"In the contest between Stupid and Evil, Stupid reaps far more destruction...all too often, Stupid is working for Evil" (Phil Rockstroh)

"I am sick of this"
(Michael Moore, writer, director, producer: Bowling for Columbine)

Welcome to our new normal. This time, the gun related massacre took place in a Milwaukee suburb of Oak Creek on August 5th, 2012. The official story is yet again that a lone gunman opened fire, this time at a Sikh temple killing six and wounding several others. A suspect who reportedly died at the scene, has been identified as Wade Michael Page, (aka Wade Vanbuskirk), an alleged neo-Nazi, active in a number of white supremacist groups. Born on Veterans Day 1971, Page joined the U.S. Army in 1992 and received a less than honorable discharge in 1998 for patterns of misconduct. It is interesting to note that he served at Fort Bragg, North Carolina as did right wing militia member Sgt. Timothy McVeigh, who was convicted of participating in the Oklahoma Bombing on April 20th, 1995. Page's supposed 9/11 American flag tattoo was a center of mainstream media focus and gave rise to speculation that this was a hate crime committed by a guy who didn't know the difference between Muslims and Sikhs and/or an incident of anti-government domestic terrorism. Strangely enough, this shooter grew up in Littleton, Colorado and attended Columbine High School, scene of the April 20th, 1999 massacre carried out by neo-Nazis Eric Harris and Dylan Klebold.

As with the Aurora gun-related tragedy there were multiple perspectives, as advocates and opponents of gun control doubled down into their respective positions. Given that this shooter's military service involved a position as "psychological operations specialist", it is not surprising that concerns were again raised as to the likelihood of it being yet another false flag operation. Critics of the official account find it unlikely that an army-trained psy-ops specialist would not know the difference between Muslims and Sikhs. As in Aurora, these doubters speculate that motives for a staged event could include an effort by Department of Homeland Security to shift their focus from foreign to domestic terrorism in order to disarm and suppress any and all opposition, and to force the population to demand "greater security" from hardline government authorities. Suspicions of this nature were fueled by multiple witness reports of four gunmen, dressed in black carrying out a well-coordinated attack involving tear gas. Other temple members had reported two suspicious men walking around their area just prior to the assault. The FBI dismissed these accounts as either irrelevant or the result of shock and confusion.

For my mind, the most interesting entry into this gridlocked discussion of gun-related violence comes from *Daily Kos* blogger Geek2's article, "Stochastic Terrorism: Triggering the Shooters", reprinted from a post on January 10th, 2011 (www.*dailykos*.com). Here the term stochastic terrorism is defined as the use of mass communications to stir up random lone wolves to carry out violent or terrorist acts that are statistically predictable, but individually unpredictable. This is a term for what emotionally-charged popular pundits such as Limbaugh, Beck, O'Reilly, Hannity, Savage, Coulter, Palin and others are lavishly paid to do on a regular basis. Any of their faithful listeners who actually plants a bomb or shoots a weapon is not a stochastic terrorist, but rather a "missile" launched into motion by stochastic terrorists who broadcast the violent memes that set them in motion. Not surprisingly, these toxic memes can and do incite unstable people to commit violent acts.

Nevertheless, stochastic terrorists succeed in maintaining their cover of plausible deniability with statements such as: "I'm not responsible for what people in my audience do". A lone wolf-missile is captured and imprisoned, if he or she survives, while these stochastic terrorists keep their prime slots as lucrative opportunities to stir their own toxic pots in order to launch even more dangerous missiles. Here, one may need to consider that a stochastic terrorist may be acting out of negligence, delusion and/or denial; rather like an intoxicated, high speed driver who runs people over without even realizing it. Or maybe these puffed up hate mongers are crazy enough to believe that they really and truly have had nothing to do with escalating the level of violence in this country. When confronted, Geek2 observes that these cowardly media celebrity-terrorists, will "duck, and weave, evade and deny, or at most offer the standard reply of 'lone nuts, Oh, so sad', but they may also let slip a subtle hint of knowledge, guilt"... or maybe even pleasure. As Geek2 says, it will happen again and again and predictably, again. "Once is a tragedy, twice a coincidence, three times is enemy action".

September 2012

Picasso's Guernica Revisited

"And at the end of all our exploring, will be to arrive where we started, and know the place for the first time." (T.S. Eliot)

The focus of this month's seminar in Mexico City is "Trauma and Relationships: Men, Women and War, and the War between Men and Women". War is one of the root causes of conflict, misunderstandings and pain between men and women and their children. Many forms of war trauma impact relationships, often for generations, and in this seminar the topic of war is expanded to include closely related issues such as violent revolutions, class war and genocide; as well as racial, religious and ethnic conflicts. For their promotional material my organizers chose the image of Picasso's, *Guernica*, created for the Spanish Republican

Pavilion at the Paris World's Fair in 1937. This now iconic, anti-war masterpiece depicts the artist's rendition of the bombing of the peaceful Basque cultural capital of Guernica on April 26, 1936, during which this entire town, (called Gernika-Lumo since 1983), was reduced to rubble. The Spanish Civil War presented Hitler with a near perfect opportunity to test Nazi plans for targeting and terrorizing civilian populations. The German dictator had loaned Fascist future dictator, Generalissimo Franco, his finest Luftwaffe Condor Legion units who were told that they were going on a "training mission." A late afternoon terror attack, during this region's market day, unleashed a hellish mixture of blast, splinter, and fire bombs. Terrified townspeople and fleeing refugees attempting to escape the mayhem, were systematically mown down by aerial strafing machine gunners. Franco then blamed the devastation on "separatist reds". Picasso's horrific mural, of these brutal war machines crushing bodies and spirits, screaming women, dead children, dismembered bodies, outrage and animal panic, now rests in Madrid's *Museo Nacional Centro de Arte Reina Sofia.*

Picasso's *Guernica* had become important to me during a much earlier time in my life before I had any thoughts of a becoming a social traumatologist. During my master's and doctoral studies in Art History at the University of California at Berkeley, I was fortunate to have Picasso expert Herschel B. Chipp (1913-1992) as my graduate advisor. As a naval lieutenant in World War II, Professor Chipp met Picasso in Paris shortly after the liberation of France and decided to devote himself to a study of his work. From a certain angle, one could almost detect a certain physical resemblance between the artist and his historian. I was also one of Herschel Chipp's teaching associates during my years of study at Berkeley and greatly benefited from his decidedly innovative methods for presenting pedagogical material. One summer when we received a grant from the Rockefeller

Foundation, we undertook a project to create multi-media slide show documentaries for undergraduate courses. (Powerpoint was not yet available). While there were other topics, most of our focus went to a presentation entitled *"Five O'Clock in the Afternoon"* which was about Picasso's *Guernica* within the historical, political and cultural context of the Spanish Civil War. Based upon a collage-like format of his canvas, black and white images from the painting were interspersed with fragments of newspaper reports of the bombing, scenes from bull fights, the Spanish *Fiesta Nacional,* Segovia's guitar music and a recitation of martyred Federico Garcia Lorca's poem about death in the afternoon, *"Lament for Ignacio Sanchez Mejias"*.

This now famous poem, so evocative of the bitter cruelties of both the Civil War and the Spanish obsession with pain and death begins as follows:

At five in the afternoon
It was exactly five in the afternoon
A boy brought a white sheet
At five in the afternoon.
A frail of lime ready prepared
At five in the afternoon.
The rest was death, and death
Alone.

Professor Chipp's gift for presenting important works of art within their historical, political and cultural context was an important inspiration for my eventual understanding of the need to see individual, social and global trauma in a similar way. The bombing of Guernica was a major social trauma which occurred within the even larger trauma of the Spanish Civil War. In recent years, my systemically oriented trauma work in Spain has clearly revealed that the still unresolved issues from that era continue to this day. In a larger sense, Picasso's *Guernica* has now come to serve as an icon of compassion for all victims of war and terror everywhere.

(For further information see: Herschel B. Chipp, *Picasso's Guernica: History, Transformations, Meaning*, University of California Press, 1988).

Aztec Sun Stone

"To us, the Aztec universe may appear irrational, terrifying, murderous in its brutality; and yet it is a mirror. Why are violence and the sacred so intertwined? Why is death seen as necessary to renew life? To hold up to our humanity, which we ignore at our cost. For in the name of other ideals and other gods, Western culture has been no less addicted to killing, even in our century." (Michael Wood, In Search of the First Civilizations)

Many visits to Mexico City's National Museum of Anthropology and History have not diminished my sense of awe in the presence of a magnificent basalt sculpture known as the Aztec Sun Stone. Located on the ground floor in the *Azteca-Mexica* exhibition hall, the museum's showpiece is around 12 feet (3.7m.) across, almost 3 feet thick and weighs around 24 tons. Often mistaken for the Mayan calendar, this circular monolith is neither Mayan nor is it a time keeping device. Various scholars estimate this grey-black solid disk was thought to have been carved sometime between 1479 and the reign of Montezuma during the early 16th century, and then buried sometime after the Spanish conquest. It was re-discovered in 1790 during excavations in the *Zocolo*, Mexico City's main central square and then mounted on a wall of their National Cathedral. Eventually, the Sun Stone arrived at the museum in 1964. The fact that 18th century scholars had referred to this circular sculpture as "Montezuma's Clock", lent credence to a mistaken idea that this, still mysterious, stone is a Pre-Colombian calendar. Such a misperception is not surprising since people that we presently refer to as Aztecs did have a round calendar which was similar, but not at all identical to a much earlier and more complex Mayan time keeping system. While these two civilizations shared a fractal understanding of time, space and transitions, along with a 260 day ritual calendar and 365 day cycle, similar to the Gregorian version, the Aztec system lacked the longer counts calculated and observed by much earlier Maya, and their even earlier Olmec predecessors.

It is important to understand that many misperceptions have plagued the well-intentioned researchers in the still developing field of Meso-American studies. First of all, the term Aztec only came into usage during the 19th century, and Mexicans never referred to themselves by that name. Moreover, the hieroglyphic script of the Maya has only been recently, and still incompletely, deciphered.

Anyone who has spent any time in pre-Columbian art and archeological circles will soon realize that, tribal warfare in these ancient civilizations is unfortunately replicated in modern academic cabals. These scholars are apt to vigorously disagree about almost anything and are often fiercely competitive, and territorial, about their own self-described theoretical territory. We need to bear this in mind as we navigate the still uncertain realms of pre-

Colombian studies. Nevertheless, it is generally agreed that the Sun Stone is so named because it contains symbols of the four "suns" or ages in Aztec cosmology, which precede our current age of the Fifth Sun. The central figure has been identified as either the Sun deity Tonatiuh, or the Earth god Tlaltecuhtli, or some combination of the two since both were believed to demand the sacrifice of human hearts and blood. Upon closer examination we can see that this figure is clearly depicted with open mouth and protruding tongue fashioned in the shape of an obsidian knife. While the Sun Stone does contain a number of astronomical symbols, its actual function was as a *cuauhxicalli,* a human sacrificial altar. In modern times, the image of the Sun Stone has become the iconic symbol for Mexico and also mistakenly for the Mayan Calendar. As such it appears on many a tourist tee-shirt and a multitude of souvenir items both worn and collected by many who are unaware of this altar's true history and significance.

October 2012

La Malinche

"After God we owe this conquest of New Spain to Doña Marina". (Hernan Cortes)

I have great respect for translators, and my international work would not be possible without their linguistic skills. Over time, I learned that I would need to understand enough of the language of the country where I am presenting in order to know if and when I am being mis-translated. Nevertheless, I have yet to become skilled enough to present in any language other than my own American English. During these international travels I have noticed that various cultures have a wide range of attitudes toward translators. In Mexico, for example, my translator for many years, a dual citizen of the USA and Mexico, equally at home in both cultures, is often treated with disrespect if not outright hostility; as she said, like a "resented outsider" or "some sort of slave". This is most interesting language and I asked her to elaborate on her fascinating systemic perspective. In Mexican history, she explained, the first translator for Cortes from Mayan to Aztec and then to Spanish, was a slave who is considered by many to be a traitor to her people.

In April 1519, conquering Spaniards were presented with 20 women servants by the defeated Mayans of Tabasco. One of these women was soon discovered to speak both Mayan and *Nahuatl,* the language of the Aztecs, and she quickly learned Spanish. Born into a noble Aztec family in 1496, she was given the name Malinali and later given over to Mayan slave traders along the Gulf Coast. Cortes arrived in 1521 and she soon found ways to move into a crucial place as his translator, secretary, cultural advisor and lover. At the time of her baptism and conversion to Christianity she took the name Marina. Aztecs addressed

Cortes as *Malinche* or "captain", and Malinali became known as *La Malinche,* "the captain's woman". Also known by the honorific title of Doña Marina, she gave birth to their son Don Martin who is considered by many to be one of the first Mestizo Mexicans of both indigenous and European ancestry. The date and circumstances of her death remain unknown although there may be reason to speculate that she died around 1551.

Now in our 21st century *La Malinche* remains a fascinating and controversial figure. According to some, she represents someone who betrayed her indigenous people to the Spaniards and the word *"malinchismo"* is a pejorative used by contemporary Mexicans to refer to fellow countrymen who prefer a way of life different from their own local culture. Others point out that she may have been the "Mother of Mexican Culture", saved many from the cruelty of the Aztecs, and even be credited with fostering Christianity throughout the New World.

Recently, feminists have portrayed *La Malinche* as a victim of forces beyond her control. Over time her image has evolved into various versions of archetype, myth and legend; as varied as the labyrinthine Mexican culture, with its ever changing social and political perspectives.

(For more information see Cypress, Sandra Messinger. *La Malinche in Mexican Literature: From History to Myth*: University of Texas Press, 1991)

November 2012

Kristallnacht

November 9-10th, 2012 mark the 74th anniversary of *Kristallnacht* or "Night of Broken Glass" in Germany and Austria. In these two countries, in 1938, the stage was set for a state sponsored Holocaust that would last until the end of World War II. This paroxysm of violence unleashed by Nazi Storm Troopers, Hitler Youth, and anti-Semitic "ordinary Germans" of all ages, resulted in a conflagration in which German Jews were beaten and humiliated; 91 died, and another 30,000 were rounded up and sent to concentration camps. As the rampage continued, German Jewish homes, schools, hospitals and businesses were looted, damaged and demolished; over a thousand synagogues were burned. (Alan E. Steinweis, *Kristallnacht*, 1938, Harvard University Press, 2009)

The following poem, "Resurrection of Jews in Germany", was written by Erik Bendix in 1989.

Erik's father Ludwig Bendix survived the Dachau concentration camp and lived to know Erik as an infant.
(www.movingmoment.com/poetry)

Unfortunately, anti-Semitism is again on the rise in Germany and other parts of Europe.

We are coming back.

Not for revenge.

Not for your sake.

Not even to prove something to God.

But because life demands it.

We do it reluctantly.

Yet we know our resistance

Will have to yield.

Our children already want to know

Why we fled our homeland,

And now try to extract justice

From Arabs who weren't even there.

They want to know

Where we lost

This God we speak of.

We want honest children,

And must admit

We have a hole in our hearts.

Back then we had to flee or die.

But now?

Excuse us, we want to pray here,

On German soil,

Where the souls of our loved ones

Still can't find any rest in the ground.

We know that your sleep

Is just as disturbed as ours,

And that you flee your own homeland

To healing spas around the globe,

That you aren't sure if foreigners

Are welcome in your country,

Perhaps because you suspect

You might no longer be welcome yourself,

That you can't answer

Your children's questions either.

Tell us, was it out of jealousy

That our loved ones were murdered?

Was the Thousand-Year Reich

And its One People

Jealous references to us,

Since Germany struggled for mere decades

To hang together,

While we did it for millennia

Using only books?

Did you gas us because

You yourselves were gassed in trenches

And then couldn't fight back?

Your thinkers now debate whether

Only European culture has come of age,

Ours about whether God still chooses us.

But are any of us talking to each other?

Our rabbis have tried for a whole generation

Never to forget,

But what stuck in memory

Was death

Which we still stare at without breathing.

To really breathe again will require living pain.

It will require that we no longer

Die witnessing,

But live fully and long.

That is what it says in our book: choose life.

In your book it says:

Love your neighbor as yourself.

We are still your neighbors.

Imagine: after a long absence,

We, your neighbors, begin to return.

Soon we'll move in next door,

And we'll stand around making noise in the streets.

Soon we'll be joking with German officials.

We'll sit at the tables for regular guests

And marry your children.

German houses and land

Will come back into our hands.

We'll be citizens again!

The empty memorial synagogues will begin to fill.

Is this a nightmare? No.

The whole world fears a recurrence,

But it is the fear that repeats itself.

The times are new.

We Jews will return to Germany.

No, not suddenly tomorrow all of us at the border.

Not next year either.

It will happen more gradually,

Here and there at first,

And then with gathering strength,

Like everything that grows.

You'll see.

December 2012

Chernobyl: As the Coffin Crumbles

"The unleashed power of the atom has changed everything save our modes of thinking, and we thus drift toward unparalleled catastrophes".
(Albert Einstein)

"The Grand Scientific Project from the time of Francis Bacon up to the Manhattan Project has been a dangerous gamble for humanity even though the advertised purpose is that progress is good".
(Richard Wilcox Ph.D., Tokyo, 2012)

We have at least some good news in that construction of a new sarcophagus designed to encase Ukraine's damaged Chernobyl nuclear reactor is finally underway. Presently funded by a multi-national consortium, the final cost is estimated to land somewhere around 1.54 billion euros (2 billion dollars). The bad news is that this gargantuan project is already a decade behind schedule and this long awaited carapace will not be ready for installation before October 2015. Meanwhile, their hastily constructed, panic stricken attempt to create some sort of emergency concrete shell, in order to entomb that still dangerous nuclear facility, has been rapidly deteriorating. An increasingly likely structural collapse could soon release tons of lethal radioactive dust into their immediate environment and also our global atmosphere. Perhaps you remember those awful events in April 1986 when the Chernobyl reactor exploded, went into meltdown, and a highly toxic radioactive plume drifted over parts of the former USSR, Eastern Europe, Scandinavia, The United Kingdom, Canada and The USA.

Vast areas from Turkey to China, the United Arab Emirates and North Africa were also exposed to a deadly, rain-out of poisons. Up until this day, and far beyond our foreseeable future, large areas of Ukraine, Belarus, and Russia remain heavily contaminated in a wake of the largest nuclear and environmental catastrophe of the 20th century. Chernobyl's radioactive emissions are considered to be 500 times more deadly than the atomic bomb we dropped over Hiroshima. Nevertheless, Russian President Vladimir Putin has announced his firm intention to proceed with his country's nuclear power plant construction programs.

In Japan, as in Russia, insanity prevails, and there is no good news from Fukushima Daiichi's damaged nuclear complex. Six reactors, three in meltdown, continue to contaminate Japan and poison the Pacific, our home world's largest ocean, as well as contaminating air, food and water throughout our entire Northern Hemisphere. The March 11, 2010 nuclear explosions, in the wake of a severe earthquake and tsunami event, which may or may not have been man made, has unleashed a situation for which there is no known solution. For various technical and other reasons, a Japanese sarcophagus designed to shield us from any of these reactors, (all built on landfill, the geological equivalent of tofu and over a seabed), is not really an option at this time, or any time in our near future. Japan is one the most seismically active regions on our planet and the precarious home to 54 nuclear reactors. Now, consider the cold hard reality that this region's ongoing quakes, which seriously endanger these reactors, are indications of a much larger geophysical movement involving unseen subterranean forces. According to Japanese environmental reporter Yoichi Shimatsu, these titanic forces are redrawing the map of the Japanese archipelago, as well as the Euro-Asian Continent and the Pacific Basin. *"Terra firma"*, he reminds us, "is an illusion. Like stones in the mud, we are deaf to the symphony of earth changes all around us". ("The Pearl Harbor Quake Was No Aftershock for Japan"). http://rense.com/general95/pearl.htm).

Despite an enormous risk of further nuclear accidents, Japan's newly elected right-wing government has announced plans to "repair" damaged nuclear installations; their clearly stated intention is to construct more of these dirty bomb facilities, as well as a nuclear weapons agenda. Nuclear insanity continues to exist, control and expand, in Russia, Japan, and anywhere else that the trans-national nuclear mafia is allowed to prevail.

Here in the USA we had a near nuclear meltdown at Pennsylvania's Three Mile Island nuclear facility in 1979. This accident is especially interesting since it was not precipitated by an earthquake, extreme weather or any other dramatic event.

In, *Normal Accidents*, sociologist Charles Perrow recounts that there was a relatively routine blockage in one of the plant's giant water filters. This caused moisture to leak into the air system, inadvertently tripping two valves which then shut down a flow of cold water into the plant's steam generator. There was a backup cooling system, but on that particular day, valves for this system were closed. Someone had closed the valves and a tag indicating this fact was blocked by another repair tag hanging from a switch above. The nuclear reactor was then left to depend upon another backup system, but again, on that particular day, the relief valve was stuck open, when it was supposed to close. And, a gauge in the control room that should have alerted operators was not working either. As a result, the reactor was close to meltdown before engineers realized what was happening. As Malcolm Gladwell points out in, *Outliers,* there was no single cause for this nuclear crisis at Three Mile Island; just five seemingly unrelated events which occurred in an unlikely sequence. If any of these malfunctions had happened in isolation, they would have caused nothing more serious than a hiccup in the system. Nevertheless, what was unlikely to happen, did happen. This is something to think about amidst the fact-resistant, pro-nuclear propaganda about the "safe, clean, green and inexpensive energy" offered by nuclear power plants.

Kafka Haunts the Airport

"The Devil himself had probably re-designed Hell in the light of information he had gained from observing airport layouts" (Anthony Price)

"Did you ever notice that the first piece of luggage on the carousel never belongs to anyone?" (Erma Bombeck)

While the Czech, German-language writer, Franz Kafka (1883-1924) lived and wrote during the last days of the Austro-Hungarian Empire, his spirit seems to live on in the modern airport experience. This author of surreal stories such as, *"The Trial"* and his unfinished *"Amerika"*, with its working title, *"The Man Who Disappeared"*, was a master of emotional suffocation and existential dread. Kafka's stories evoke a struggle for existence in a mysteriously antagonistic world where one is likely to be suspected of some undetermined crime by some remote, inaccessible authority. His themes of frustration, alienation, and futility, in ongoing attempts to engage absurd bureaucracies, became vivid reality during my own attempts to obtain a much needed boarding pass at the check-in counter at the airport in Buenos Aires. As it turned out, this was only the beginning of yet another Kafkaesque travel adventure.

My return ticket to the USA involved a *LAN Chile* flight from Argentina to Santiago de Chile where I was to catch a connecting flight with *American Airlines* to Dallas-Fort Worth, and then two more connections via *U.S. Airways*. At the *LAN* counter they cheerfully checked my baggage all the way through to my final destination, and then refused to issue boarding passes for any flight other than theirs to Santiago. While *American* and *LAN* have supposedly merged, *LAN* refused to issue a boarding pass for my *American* flight which they claimed could only be issued by *AA*. And so, I made my way to the far end the terminal and patiently waited in yet another queue for an opportunity to speak with an agent at an *American Airline*s counter, only to be told, some 30 minutes later, that their boarding pass could only be issued by *LAN*. And so, I flew on to Chile in the hope that airlines there would be more co-operative. While the *AA* agent in Santiago was willing to issue a pass to board my flight to Texas, she refused to issue passes for any remaining connections. As compensation, I was issued a very small square of paper resembling my luggage receipt, which this agent assured me would allow me to obtain a boarding document at the *US Airways* departure gate.

After a total of 15 hours of flying, and more of those infernal airport queues, I arrived at Dallas-Fort Worth in a somewhat disoriented travel haze. Ubiquitous fluorescent lighting made certain that I was looking more and more like my passport photo. With less than an hour to catch my next flight, the TSA lady at the head of a security line, apparently channeling Kafka, just laughed when I showed her my small square of "document" issued in Chile. Needless to say, she refused any attempt to approach any gate from her well-guarded post. Even worse, I soon learned that *US Air* was actually located in a distant terminal that would now require a trip by shuttle bus. My next challenge in this labyrinth of frustration was to locate both of the airport's shuttle stops as well as exactly the right bus. After being given a series of wrong directions I found myself in an elevator with a kindly soul who offered to help.

Dressed in the Hunter Green sports coat of an airport volunteer he was one of the many angels in human form who donate their time and energy to assist countless lost souls who find themselves wandering in the Stygian nightmare of modern air travel. My celestial guide knew how to locate the right route to my terminal shuttle bus. As we boarded together, he explained that the terminal at our destination was under construction and therefore we would need to walk the final quarter mile. With the clock running, my pulse racing and blood pressure rising, we arrived at the *US Air* counter where my angel moved me right to the head of the line. The majority of these airport angels are senior citizens, with enough life experience and acquired patience to enable them to deal effectively with overwrought travelers; and there are a desperate lot of us.

Precious boarding passes were quickly issued as I took off on an angst-ridden dash toward my departure gate and those inevitable proto-military protocols of our supposedly patriotic Transport Security Administration. This much reviled, dystopian agency appeared soon after the still controversial events of 9/11. TSA's inflexible, inquisitional, interactive style, apparently designed as a form of obedience training, has won few admirers within the traveling public, who have vociferously complained to their congressional representatives, and to absolutely no avail. Just recently, John Pistole, head of TSA, a congressionally funded federal agency, refused to appear before a congressional investigating committee while stating that his agency was not subject to their federal oversight inquiries. Kafka would have understood both the mindset of congress and Pistole's reasoning.

As a general rule, I have avoided TSA's naked-body, back-scatter x-ray machines since I receive more than enough radiation flying through jet streams in this post-Fukushima world. Claims that these scanners are "safe" have failed to convince. Medical x-ray devices have been known to seriously malfunction, with lethal results, and I don't see why these airport machines, operated by marginally trained personnel, should be any different. As much as I dislike this "above the law" federal agency, I am concerned for the health and welfare of their low paid workers (and their offspring and other loved ones) whose job requires them to remain in close proximity to these potentially cancer causing and fertility-damaging x-ray emitters. After a substantial public outcry these infernal devices are finally being removed from major airports only to be inflicted on smaller local installations. In their place, we now find the latest scanning device which is also purported to be "safe", as I soon discovered on my dash to a seemingly elusive boarding gate.

Dallas-Fort Worth has recently installed one of these newer scanning devices, which looks something like an oversize glass telephone booth. Travelers are expected to approach these millimeter wave imaging machines with shoes removed, along with belts, jewelry and pockets emptied. Once inside this booth one is ordered to stand, raise arms above the head in the universal gesture of surrender, while being subjected to low energy radio waves similar to cell phone emissions. Normally I would choose their "opt out" option for an intrusive pat down, since I am more willing to be groped than x-rayed, or in this case microwaved. However, time was of the essence and I agreed to be scanned for the first, and I hope, last time by this insufficiently tested device. As it turned out, I made it to my *US Air* departure gate just as they were boarding my flight. While I would like to believe that the spirit of Franz Kafka is limited to airports, here in the USA, aided by surveillance drones and hidden cameras, TSA is busy expanding their "security operations" to bus, subway and train stations, as well as random check points set up along our highways.

Toxic Cloud over Buenos Aires

"The safety of the people shall be the highest law".
(Cicero)

Overall, I have been quite fortunate throughout my international travels with both timing and safety concerns and have also benefited from "travel mercies" received from a prayer chain organized by my Mother's church. Good fortune prevailed once again in the timing of my recent departure from *Buenos Aires*. Just the day before leaving, I had arrived at their central port on the *Rio de la Plata* aboard a ferry from Uruguay and then departed by plane on Tuesday, December 4th, arriving in the USA on Wednesday December 5th. Safely home again, with my usual jet lag, unable to sleep, I turned to my computer in the early morning hours and found startling news of a toxic event in the Argentine capital on Thursday, December 6th.

In a scene worthy of a disaster film, a shipping container docked at the central port's terminal four, had apparently either exploded or caught fire. The resulting billow of smoke diffused out into the city, whose name means "good air", in the form of a foul smelling, sulfurous, yellow smog extending to a distance of at least 15 kilometers (about 9 miles). An emergency alert advised an alarmed populace to remain indoors, close windows and doors and turn off air conditioning in an already uncomfortably hot and humid morning. Areas within a 20 block radius of the port were evacuated amidst the area's legendary nightmare of noise and traffic congestion. While many were taken to soon overwhelmed hospitals, many others, struggling to concoct makeshift masks with scarves and other material, were also suffering from eye irritation, nausea, vomiting, and complaining of respiratory difficulties.

All decked out in a hazmat suit, Security Minister Sergio Berni assured the public that the container contained a phosphorous-based pesticide of "low toxicity", especially since it was so diluted. This is a less than re-assuring pronouncement from someone who feels a need to wear full-out hazardous material protective gear. Nevertheless, his predictable message seems to be derived from a nearly universal formula for officials withholding information vital to public health out of concern "to avoid panic". According to the Ministry of Health, the technical name of the offending pesticide is Thiodicarb, made in China, and this particular shipment was on its way to Paraguay. At the time of the toxic dispersion this container was being held in a section of the river port reserved for hazardous cargo. There are further reports alleging that there are 35 containers holding exactly the same chemical still remaining in that location.

(Jonathan Gilbert, *U.K. Telegraph*, 12/06/2012).

Minister Berni's assessment of Thiodicarb's "low toxicity" remains open to question. According to Bayer Crop Science, this product contains a petroleum distillate moderately to highly toxic to fish and other aquatic life in lakes, streams or ponds. This is especially unfortunate given that this accident occurred along the *Rio de la Plata* which runs along the border between Argentina and Uruguay. Thiodicarb also contains Endosulfan, (Hexachlorohexahydromethano-2,4,3-benzodioxanthiepin-oxide) which may impact the central nervous system. Symptoms of poisoning include nausea, vomiting, headache, general malaise, and breathing problems. Children and pets are especially vulnerable. Bayer's first aid advice includes calling a doctor or a poison control center immediately, rinsing the eyes for 15-20 minutes, and removing contact lenses. Contaminated clothing should be removed and laundered and leather shoes discarded. Hair and skin surfaces should be immediately rinsed with plenty of water for 15-

20 minutes and those who have inhaled Thiodicarb should be immediately removed to fresh air and given artificial respiration if necessary. (www.cropgro.org)

The ongoing possibility for events such as this, is yet another reason to travel with a highly effective respiratory mask and keep extras in your vehicle for yourself and other passengers. Ever since Japan's March 11, 2010 nuclear disaster, I have taken the advice of environmental reporter Michael Collins (www.enviroreporter.com), and brought along my Nano-Mask with disposable filters for air travel. As he and many others say, the jet stream in the northern hemisphere is increasingly and ongoingly radioactive. My husband tests these filters with our radiation counter when I return and results so far have registered at least double the background levels of radiation. Nano-masks are available from www.emergencyfiltration.com. In areas where they are not available, avian flu masks offer an alternative.

In the case of air-borne radiation, chemicals, and other toxins, flimsy paper masks provide only minimal protection.

December 7th brought further mayhem to *Buenos Aires* in the form an intense, torrential downpour which delivered the worst flooding in over half a century. There were power outages, the city's transport network was nearly at a standstill, and much of the city's financial and commercial activities were suspended. Nothing to worry about however, authorities assured everyone that "everything is under control". (*Russian Television*, 12/07/2012).

It Can't Happen Here....

"That men do not learn very much from history is the most important of all lessons of history".
(Aldous Huxley)

I have just finished reading Frances Itani's: *Requiem,* about the round up and internment of Canadians of Japanese descent, following the bombing of Pearl Harbor. There is much wisdom within this beautifully written novel about resilience and the healing power of community, as well as the emotional cost of suppression. Many alive today are both unaware of this episode in Canadian history and also quite convinced that such a thing could never happen here in our United States of America. After all, any looming prospect of concentration camps here in America belongs only to the realm of conspiracy theorists, because our freedoms are guaranteed by our constitution, and therefore, "it can't happen here". Yes, theoretically, but the historical truth is that it has *already* happened here. After the Pearl Harbor attack of December 7, 1941, President Franklin D. Roosevelt issued executive order #9066 authorizing the creation of what he termed "concentration camps".

With the aid of the U.S. Census Bureau's supposedly confidential information, hundreds of thousands of Japanese and people of Japanese descent were summarily rounded up, taken from their homes and places of work, and transported to various government facilities. Often, with only the clothes on their backs, they were herded into Assembly Centers and then transported, by truck, bus, or train to Re-Location Centers, and from there into Internment Camps. Families were compelled to subsist in overcrowded, hastily constructed, tar paper covered barracks, with inadequate heat, nutrition or medical care. Those considered to be of special interest to the government were moved along into more draconian Detention Camps. All of these facilities, which operated in bleak, remote locations, under consistently grim, sub-standard conditions, were surrounded by barbed wire and armed guards.

Over 62% of the 160,000 detainees were American citizens; most others were legally registered aliens, and the majority were children of school age or under.

When I was working at a medical clinic in Colorado one of my older patients had a vivid dream that he could speak Japanese. This was so disturbing for him that we decided to look deeper into this experience. Eventually, it transpired that his father had been a commandant at one of the Japanese internment camps in southeastern Colorado. As a boy, he was allowed to play with Japanese kids and they were there long enough for him to become conversationally fluent in their language. He remembered these Japanese as friends and soon came to remember why he had needed to forget.

In 1945 most Japanese detainees were released into a post-war reality where their previous wealth, possessions, or livelihood had been lost or destroyed. Many suffered ongoing health and psychological problems and an unshakeable sense of shame, in the aftermath of internment.

More about this disgraceful episode in American history is available in, *Years of Infamy*, by Michi Weglyn and James A. Michener, (University of Washington Press, 1976).

Perhaps there is some comfort in the fact that the U.S. government eventually passed legislation apologizing for this internment. The legislation signed by Ronald Reagan in 1988, expressed regret for "actions based on a race prejudice, war hysteria and failure of political leadership". Having finally to come to their senses, one would imagine that our political leaders and fellow countrymen would never allow another episode of this nature to take place on American soil. Then again, one might be well advised to take notice of

251

the latest development in our so-called "War on Terror", supposedly justified by the events of September 11, 2001. Now in December of 2011, members of both Congress and the Senate, with minimal debate or discussion, have passed legislation that authorizes our military to arrest and *indefinitely detain* any American citizen, without trial or right to even know anything about the charges against them. This news arrives in concert with government and Department of Justice contracts recently issued to Halliburton subsidiaries, to activate the 600 Federal Emergency Management Agency camps located throughout our 50 states. What, one then might ask, is this emergency that mandates activation of these nation-wide FEMA camps? Social Unrest? Domestic Terrorists?

Perhaps we should take a closer look at our citizens, now subject to indefinite detention, who are suspected of being terrorists. According to recent memos issued by Homeland Security and our Department of Justice, suspects include those in possession of "ready to eat meals", storage of more than a seven day supply of food, weather proof ammunition, brightly colored stains on clothing, paying in cash or change in hair color. Janet Napolitano is decidedly uncomfortable with activists of any ilk; especially those concerned with immigration, New World Order as a threat, abortion, animal rights, 9/11 truth, birth certificates, environmental issues, compulsory vaccination, negative view of the UN, anti-war causes, and anyone involved in Occupy Wall Street protests. Special concern is apparently warranted toward anyone with missing fingers or other body parts. These folks are likely to be Afghan or Iraq war veterans who are now considered to be a danger to their homeland. We are also advised to be on the alert for anyone with a shaved head who purchases night vision equipment; such as goggles or a flashlight, drives vehicles with bumper stickers supporting third party candidates, espouses radical theology, or emits "strange odors".

In all likelihood it would seem that many of these domestic terror suspects could be readily identified at your local Walmart. In case you forget, a video message from Big Sis is there at the check-out counter to remind you... "If you see something, say something". Reporting these alleged undesirables to Homeland Security is especially convenient now that our protectors have likely parked their vans and/or mobile surveillance towers just outside in the nearby parking lot...for your safety and convenience, of course.

There is nothing at all to worry about for those of us who would never, ever expect to find ourselves in any of the above categories of suspicion. Just in case, however, it might be prudent to re-visit this now iconic warning from Pastor Martin Niemoller:

First they came for the Socialists, and I did not speak out-
Because I was not a Socialist.
Then they came for the Trade Unionists, and I did not speak out-
Because I was not a Trade Unionist.

Then they came for the Jews, and I did not speak out –
Because I was not a Jew.
Then they came for me- and there was no one left to speak for me.

They did come for him and he spent seven years in a concentration camp. More about Pastor Niemoller's life is available in the biography by James Bentley, *Martin Niemoller 1892-1984,* (NY Macmillan Free Press, 1984).

Some Comfort in Newton/ Sandy Hook

"I think we're a very frightened people"
(Michael Moore, December, 2012)

This holiday season arrived with yet another heart shattering, gun-related massacre. Please keep in mind that with this and other similar tragedies, corporate controlled media reports are often erroneous...and that things are not always what they seem. Now is a time for grief and reflection. Uncovering the many layers of this complex event requires patience, and hidden systemic elements may only come into focus over time. Unlike our other gun-related mass murder episodes, my sense is that the inexorable tragedy of the Sandy Hook Elementary School massacre may represent a cultural tipping point in American's relationship with their firearms...at least within our legal system. And, to some limited extent, changes may be brewing within the mass media, video game, entertainment, and pharmacological industries.

One small bright spot appeared in the grief-stricken Connecticut community with the arrival of gentle, Golden Retriever, comfort dogs whose mission in life is to help people feel better. As the trainer of this team of canines from the Lutheran Church Charities explained, "These dogs are non-judgmental. They are loving. They are accepting of anyone". For several hours they drew grateful attention at a teddy-bear memorial set up near the town Christmas tree. Many locals, visitors, journalists and even crews from multiple satellite trucks, paused and took time to stroke these soft, furry, "emotional counselors". Comfort dogs understand the power of loving presence. They don't ask anyone to describe their feelings when there just are no words; and dogs never say the wrong thing.

Therapy animals are used in a number of programs across the country. Organizations such as the ASPCA and Pet Partners, offer training for pet owners who would like to volunteer their animals for service to people in need; cancer support groups, autistic children, elder and nursing care homes, the disabled and victims of tragedy. In my own experience of working with traumatized people, animals have often been an important resource. While I was in private practice, my own animals would sometimes attend certain sessions. Clients were always welcome to bring their own pets and many of them often did. Dogs have also been welcome visitors to my international seminars and some of them even became "regulars". (Agence France-Presse, "Dogs help Newton residents cope with tragedy").

(http://www.rawstory.com/rs/2012).

(Mary Elizabeth Williams, www.salon.com, 12/18/2012).

CONCLUSION

"Life moves on whether we act as cowards or heroes. Life has no other discipline to impose, if we but realize it. Everything we shut our eyes to, we run away from, everything we deny, denigrate or despise serves to defeat us in the end. What seems nasty, painful, even evil, can become a source of beauty, joy and strength, if faced with an open mind. (Henry Miller)

Given that there is no shortage of trauma here in our modern world, one of my most frequently asked questions is: "How can relatives, friends, loved ones and concerned others, be of support and assistance to someone living with the consequences of unresolved trauma". Offering support can be quite challenging because post-traumatic symptoms can appear under a guise of many seemingly unrelated behaviors; depression, grandiosity, suicide attempts, addictions, eating disorders, chronic pain, compulsive busyness, extreme sports, panic attacks, violence, religious or political fanaticism, sexual acting out, blind devotion to a self-described mission, obsessive need to rescue and/or control, and any other self-destructive behavior.

Any, all or some combination of the above conditions may be an attempt at a form of self-medication in order to handle something or many things which may be just too much to bear. Trauma survivors may also experience a compulsion to re-enact a trauma or some aspect of a trauma in some form, along with an inability to perceive any options other than repeating destructive behavior. Needless to say this can be deeply distressing, even dangerous for the traumatized as well as those who love and care for them. It is not unusual for trauma survivors to enter into a trauma bond; which can be understood as a dynamic enmeshment with others who have been overwhelmed in a similar manner or event. These trauma bonds can form within intimate relationships, giving the illusion of finding something like a "soul mate", who is in reality a "wound mate". Such relationships survive only when both remain wounded. Trauma survivors may also seek comfort and kinship with members of a support group, military unit, religious affiliation, political party, clan, tribe, race or gender preference, who suffer from similar traumas. In the short term, these affiliations may indeed offer much needed understanding and solace. The danger, however, is that extended enmeshment in these trauma bonds, together with other survivors; tend to isolate one from friends, family, and others who have not shared the same, exact, overwhelming experience.

We see trauma bonding very clearly dramatized in the movie, *Fearless;* a true story about the United Airlines, Sioux City air disaster, starring Jeff Bridges. As the story unfolds it becomes clear that survivors have formed trauma bonds and only want to be with each other, and therefore are no longer interested nor able to relate to others not involved in the crash. As a result of such trauma bonding, personal and professional relationships are lost; and families may fragment, be disturbed, and lose a sense of cohesiveness. Here it needs to be said that entire families, religions, cults, races and nations, with the help of their leaders and their chosen controlled media outlets, can also be caught and manipulated in these delusional entanglements.

Trauma bonds are re-enforced by a belief that the only hope for any sense of safety lies within a survivor's, often narrow, emotional confines, and that the outside world is dangerous and not to be trusted. While there are situations in which there may be some very real truth to this perception, and therefore it cannot be entirely discounted, this viewpoint also presents a serious limitation for those who seek recovery. Concerned friends, who truly want to help, need to know that it is vitally important not to over-react, function with excessive caretaking, or treat your loved one as a poor, helpless victim. This attitude is demeaning, sends a message of weakness, fosters dependence, and might just provoke an angry or even explosive response.

Trauma survivors need to maintain or even find their own way back to self-respect, dignity and empowerment. It is important to recognize that there is more than one path to recovery.

Over time I have come to understand that encouraging or even insisting that overwhelmed people re-live their experiences and talk about painful feelings is counter-productive. Such an approach runs the risk of generating ongoing cycles of re-traumatization. It is vitally important never to do anything to overwhelm an already overwhelmed individual, family, community or other social system. For those who wish to be of assistance, our primary task is to find existing and potential resources and ways to establish contact with the traumatized person or group; to restore some sense of connection to self and others and move in the direction of balance. There are those who still believe that acute shock and ongoing trauma states are only in the mind; but the reality is that there a strong somatic component as well. Very simple, gentle, somatic interventions based upon easily transmitted concepts, can provide much needed first aid in acute and chronic situations. Most important is not to rush into doing something, or practicing some questionable technique, before one even has a clear sense of who you are working with and what is really going on. The current fad for mass marketed protocols for treating only symptoms, serves to perpetuate the mechanistic and outdated Cartesian illusion that human beings are biological machines in need of "fixing". This atomistic and seriously disconnected view of human suffering has little to offer a soul's need for wholeness; and the careful re-connection to self, others, and the greater forces within our environmental matrix.

The human need for wholeness involves the need to be seen as a whole person; an integral part of a family, clan and even larger system, and not just some embodied collection of symptoms. A basic rule of ecology is that everything is connected to everything else. If one can accept this, then a systemic approach to understanding and resolving trauma has much to offer.

From my perspective, the essential goal of trauma work is to find ways to expand, to include, and then to become larger than whatever has happened to us. It has been my experience that trauma is not something that can be fixed or that one can completely get over. Overwhelming life experiences are integral to who we are and who we can and will become. The challenge then becomes: how to find ways to expand, to include and grow larger than whatever has happened to us.

In the natural world, for example, one can find the history of trees exactly described within their ring patterns, and there are marine shells that encase and display their changing relationship with the sea. I believe that we are rather like tree rings and shell patterns, in that, the events that happen to us, as well as our responses to those events, leave a permanent record within the larger pattern of our lives. The goal of trauma recovery therefore, is not to erase or cure. If one thinks of integrating and resolving, rather than eliminating traumatic experience, then there is the possibility to bring the human organism, in all of its dimensions, back into a state of balance and resiliency.

Made in the USA
San Bernardino, CA
16 May 2013